Practice Book

Teacher Edition
Grade 2

☰Harcourt School Publishers

www.harcourtschool.com

ISBN 10: 0-15-349883-8
ISBN 13: 978-0-15-349883-1

1 2 3 4 5 6 7 8 9 10 073 17 16 14 13 12 11 10 09 08 07

Contents

ROLLING ALONG

BLAST OFF!

Contents

ROLLING ALONG

BLAST OFF!

Practice Book
© Harcourt • Grade 2

Name _____

▶ Circle the word that completes each sentence.

1. Pat put a _____ on the letter.
   lamp (stamp) stump

2. The _____ waved on the pole.
   (flag) flat flip

3. Anna _____ very fast in the race.
   rat (ran) rip

4. Juan likes to _____ in the big chair.
   sack sip (sit)

5. The cook put food on the _____.
   wish dash (dish)

6. Al felt so _____ he wanted to cry.
   (sad) sap tap

7. The hungry cat looked _____.
   chin (thin) chat

8. Cal wrote a _____ of books to read.
   (list) last fist

School-Home Connection
Have your child read aloud all the words that he or she circled. Then have your child use each word in a sentence.

Practice Book
© Harcourt • Grade 2

Name _____

▶ Read the Spelling Words. Sort the words and write them where they belong.

Order may vary.

Words with short _a_

Spelling Words
flag
fin
ran
has
fill
sat
list
sit
bag
win

1. flag
2. ran
3. has
4. sat
5. bag

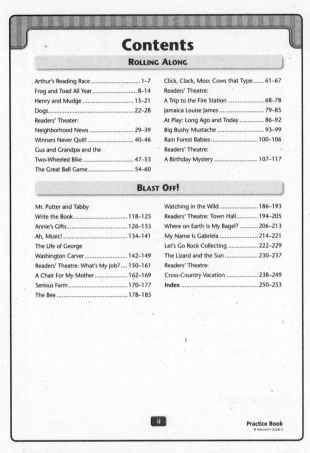

Words with short _i_

6. fin
7. fill
8. list
9. sit
10. win

School-Home Connection
Ask your child why he or she wrote the Spelling Words in each part of the chart. Help your child brainstorm other words that have the short vowel a or i sound.

Practice Book
© Harcourt • Grade 2

Name _____

▶ Read the story. Then complete the character chart. Write the ending of each sentence.

Frieda's Day at the Beach

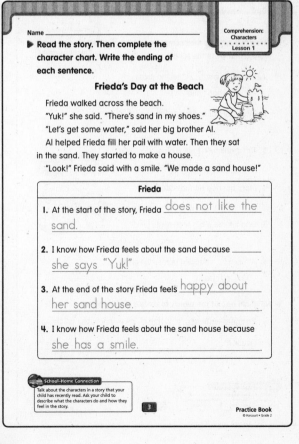

Frieda walked across the beach.
"Yuk!" she said. "There's sand in my shoes."
"Let's get some water," said her big brother Al.
Al helped Frieda fill her pail with water. Then they sat in the sand. They started to make a house.
"Look!" Frieda said with a smile. "We made a sand house!"

Frieda
1. At the start of the story, Frieda does not like the sand.
2. I know how Frieda feels about the sand because she says "Yuk!"
3. At the end of the story Frieda feels happy about her sand house.
4. I know how Frieda feels about the sand house because she has a smile.

School-Home Connection
Talk about the characters in a story that your child has recently read. Ask your child to describe what the characters do and how they feel in the story.

Practice Book
© Harcourt • Grade 2

© Harcourt • Grade 2

Student Edition pp. ii–3

▶ **Circle the word that completes each
sentence. Write the word on the line.**

1. Jack put his lunch in a __bag__.

   big (bag) bat

2. Ana __ran__ to catch the bus.

   (ran) rim ram

3. I do not want to __tip__ the boat over.

   (tip) trip risk

4. Sara tried hard to __win__ the bicycle race.

   fan fin (win)

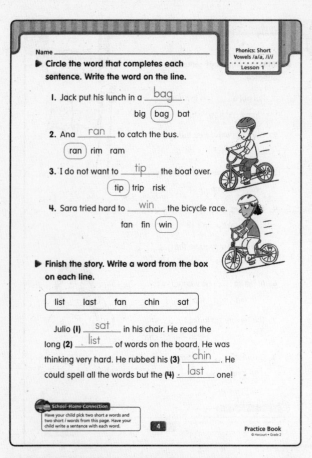

▶ **Finish the story. Write a word from the box
on each line.**

| list | last | fan | chin | sat |

Julio **(1)** __sat__ in his chair. He read the
long **(2)** __list__ of words on the board. He was
thinking very hard. He rubbed his **(3)** __chin__. He
could spell all the words but the **(4)** __last__ one!

School-Home Connection
Have your child pick two short a words and
two short i words from this page. Have your
child write a sentence with each word.
4

▶ **Write a word from the box that completes
each sentence.**

| prove | already | sign | eight | police |

1. Jen had __already__ read the story.

2. The __police__ make sure you are safe.

3. I can read the street __sign__.

4. Jim ran hard to __prove__ he was fast.

5. The number after seven is __eight__.

▶ **Write an answer to each question on the lines.**

6. How do the **police** help people stay safe?

   Possible response: They stop people who

   drive too fast.

7. How could you **prove** you were fast?

   Possible response: I could beat someone in

   a race.

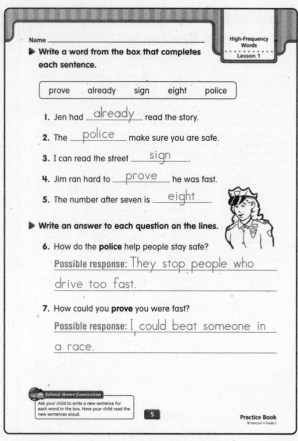

School-Home Connection
Ask your child to write a new sentence for
each word in the box. Have your child read the
new sentences aloud.
5

▶ **Circle the syllable that completes each
word. Then write the letters on the line.**

1. We had a pic __nic__ on the grass.

   nap (nic) nip

2. Mom got hot dogs out of the bas __ket__.

   (ket) bit roc

3. Tim drank milk from a plas __tic__ cup.

   zim bag (tic)

4. Mom handed Pam a nap __kin__.

   tab rip (kin)

5. Dad bit into a big bran muf __fin__.

   nap mug (fin)

6. A rab __bit__ hopped across the grass.

   kin (bit) top

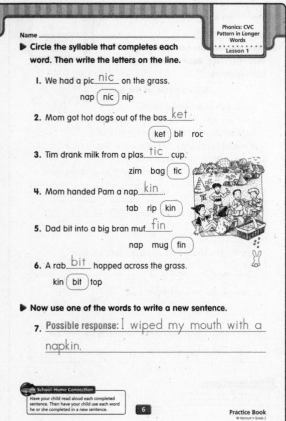

▶ **Now use one of the words to write a new sentence.**

7. **Possible response:** I wiped my mouth with a

   napkin.

School-Home Connection
Have your child read aloud each completed
sentence. Then have your child use each word
he or she completed in a new sentence.
6

▶ **Read each group of words. If the group
is a sentence, write** *sentence* **on the line.
If it is not a sentence, write** *no.*

1. I see a frog. __sentence__

2. jumped the frog in the water __no__

3. Pat sat on the rug. __sentence__

4. Ann and Dan can run fast. __sentence__

5. cakes and cookies __no__

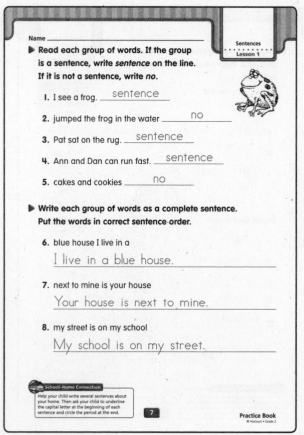

▶ **Write each group of words as a complete sentence.
Put the words in correct sentence order.**

6. blue house I live in a

   I live in a blue house.

7. next to mine is your house

   Your house is next to mine.

8. my street is on my school

   My school is on my street.

School-Home Connection
Help your child write several sentences about
your home. Then ask your child to underline
the capital letter at the beginning of each
sentence and circle the period at the end.
7

Student Edition pp. 4–7

© Harcourt • Grade 2

Name _____

▶ Circle the word that completes each sentence.

1. Tomás felt very _____ in the sun.
   (hot)   hat   hut

2. The _____ is full of milk.
   mall   (mug)   met

3. The chair has a broken _____.
   log   lug   (leg)

4. The _____ is crawling in the grass.
   beg   bog   (bug)

5. Sam had two fish in her _____!
   nut   not   (net)

6. Sonya put the _____ on her foot.
   sick   (sock)   stack

7. There is food in the _____.
   (pot)   put   pat

8. I like cats _____ Mom likes dogs.
   bat   bit   (but)

9. My _____ is a bird.
   (pet)   pot   pod

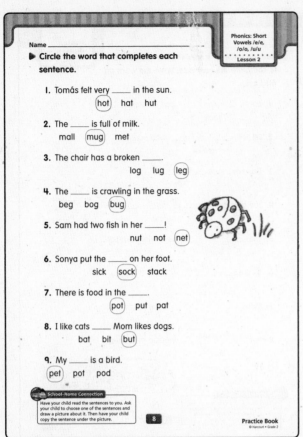

Name _____

▶ Read the Spelling Words. Sort the words and write them where they belong.
Order may vary.

Words with Short e

1. best
2. bed
3. get
4. ten

Words with Short o

5. not
6. job
7. spot

Words with Short u

8. run
9. mud
10. duck

Spelling Words

not
best
run
bed
spot
get
mud
ten
duck
job

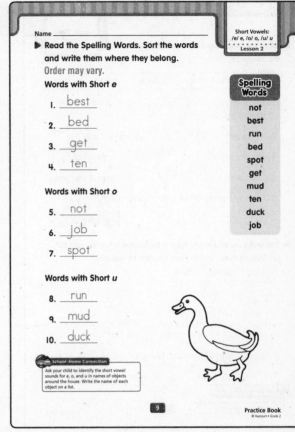

Name _____

▶ Read the story. Then complete the sentences in the chart to tell about the characters.

At the Pet Store

Jen and Alexa are friends. Jen has long brown hair. Alexa has short red hair. The girls like going to the pet store.

"The hamsters are the best," says Alexa. "They are so cute!"

"No, the snakes are the best," says Jen.

"Look at the birds!" says Alexa. "I want a bird!"

"Me too!" says Jen.

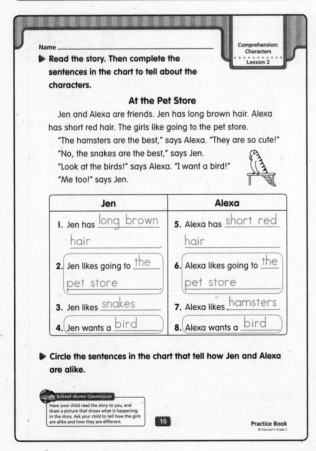

Jen	Alexa
1. Jen has long brown hair	5. Alexa has short red hair
2. Jen likes going to the pet store	6. Alexa likes going to the pet store
3. Jen likes snakes	7. Alexa likes hamsters
4. Jen wants a bird	8. Alexa wants a bird

▶ Circle the sentences in the chart that tell how Jen and Alexa are alike.

Name _____

▶ Finish the story. On each line, write a word from the box.

| hop | bed | get | mud |
| not | wet | mug | |

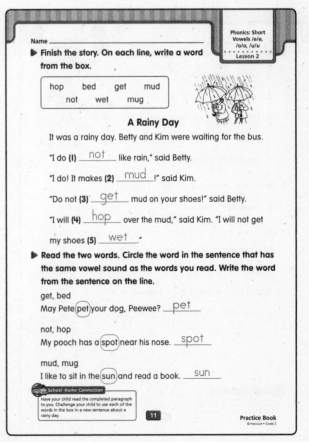

A Rainy Day

It was a rainy day. Betty and Kim were waiting for the bus.

"I do (1) not like rain," said Betty.

"I do! It makes (2) mud !" said Kim.

"Do not (3) get mud on your shoes!" said Betty.

"I will (4) hop over the mud," said Kim. "I will not get my shoes (5) wet ."

▶ Read the two words. Circle the word in the sentence that has the same vowel sound as the words you read. Write the word from the sentence on the line.

get, bed
May Pete (pet) your dog, Peewee? pet

not, hop
My pooch has a (spot) near his nose. spot

mud, mug
I like to sit in the (sun) and read a book. sun

Student Edition pp. 8–11

Name _____

▶ Write the word from the box that completes the sentence.

| covered | everything | through | woods | guess |

1. Tara tried to _____guess_____ how many beans were in the jar.

2. Arturo put _____everything_____ on the table.

3. The dog jumped _____through_____ the hoop.

4. The storm _____covered_____ the ground with snow.

5. Carla saw many different trees in the _____woods_____.

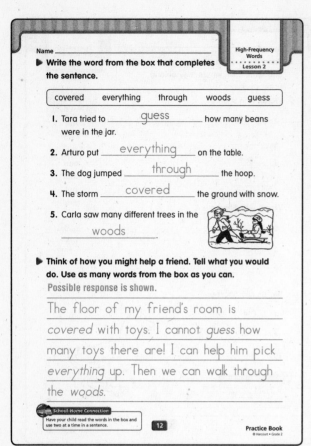

▶ Think of how you might help a friend. Tell what you would do. Use as many words from the box as you can.

Possible response is shown.

The floor of my friend's room is _covered_ with toys. I cannot _guess_ how many toys there are! I can help him pick _everything_ up. Then we can walk through the _woods_.

School-Home Connection
Have your child read the words in the box and use two at a time in a sentence.

12

Name _____

▶ Add the ending -s or -es to the base word to complete the sentence. Write the word on the line.

1. Gil's _____socks_____ don't match!
   sock

2. Fill five _____glasses_____ with milk.
   glass

3. This shop sells _____watches_____.
   watch

4. The girls got new _____dresses_____.
   dress

5. The _____boxes_____ were filled with pots.
   box

6. All the _____dishes_____ are in the sink.
   dish

7. Many _____frogs_____ live in the pond.
   frog

8. Ten _____buses_____ went up the street.
   bus

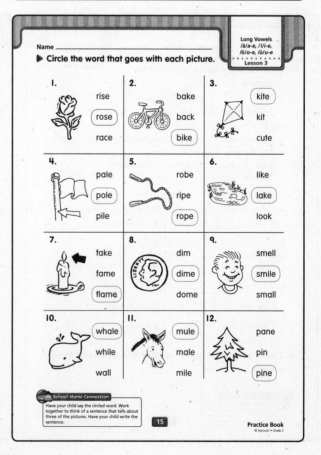

School-Home Connection
Write the words pot, fox, inch, job, duck, wish, fin, and bench on a piece of paper. Have your child add the ending -s or -es to these base words. Discuss your child's answers.

13

Name _____

▶ Write the correct end mark on the line.

1. Where are you going __?__

2. I am going to a birthday party ____

3. The party is for my friend Anna ____

4. Do you know how old she is __?__

5. She is eight years old ____

▶ Write each sentence correctly.

6. i have two brothers
   I have two brothers.

7. i have one sister
   I have one sister.

8. do you have any brothers or sisters
   Do you have any brothers or sisters?

School-Home Connection
Ask your child to explain the difference between statements and questions. Take turns asking questions and answering with statements.

14

Name _____

▶ Circle the word that goes with each picture.

1.	rise / **rose** / race	2.	bake / back / **bike**	3.	**kite** / kit / cute
4.	pale / **pole** / pile	5.	robe / ripe / **rope**	6.	like / **lake** / look
7.	fake / fame / **flame**	8.	dim / **dime** / dome	9.	smell / **smile** / small
10.	**whale** / while / wall	11.	**mule** / male / mile	12.	pane / pin / **pine**

School-Home Connection. Have your child say the circled word. Work together to think of a sentence that tells about three of the pictures. Have your child write the sentence.

15

Name _____

Long Vowels:
/ā/ a-e, /ī/ i-e,
/ō/ o-e, /ū/u-e
Lesson 3

▶ Make two cards for each Spelling Word.
Lay them down and read them. Write each
word where it belongs.

1. Write the words *with* long vowel *a*.
2. Write the words *with* long vowel *i*.
3. Write the words *with* long vowel *o*.
4. Write the words *with* long vowel *u*.

Spelling Words

same
kite
home
plate
ride
rope
race
rule
broke
tune

Words with Long *a*	Words with Long *i*
same	kite
plate	ride
race	

Words with Long *o*	Words with Long *u*
home	rule
rope	tune
broke	

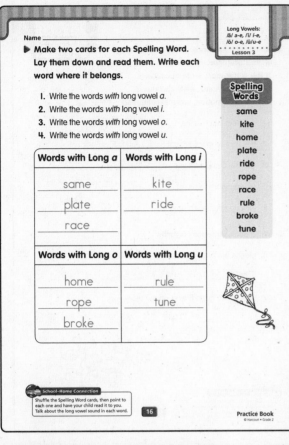

16

▶ Read the paragraph. Write the supporting
details on the lines.

Caring for a Rabbit

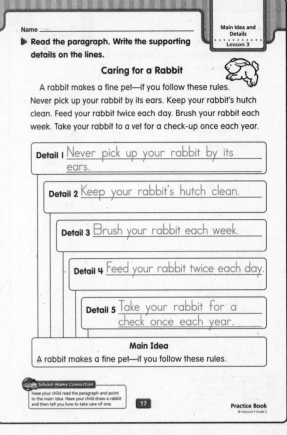

A rabbit makes a fine pet—if you follow these rules.
Never pick up your rabbit by its ears. Keep your rabbit's hutch
clean. Feed your rabbit twice each day. Brush your rabbit each
week. Take your rabbit to a vet for a check-up once each year.

Detail 1 Never pick up your rabbit by its ears.

Detail 2 Keep your rabbit's hutch clean.

Detail 3 Brush your rabbit each week.

Detail 4 Feed your rabbit twice each day.

Detail 5 Take your rabbit for a check once each year.

Main Idea
A rabbit makes a fine pet—if you follow these rules.

17

Name _____

Long Vowels
/ā/a-e, /ī/i-e,
/ō/o-e, /ū/u-e
Lesson 3

▶ Finish the story. On each line, write a word
from the box.

face	stroke	home	cage	nice
name	size	huge	time	rode

A Pet for June

June and her dad went to get a pet. June saw a big
white dog.

"He's too (1) _huge_," said Dad. "We need a dog
that is a smaller (2) _size_."

June stuck her hand inside the white dog's

(3) _cage_. The big dog came over and licked her

(4) _face_. June began to (5) _stroke_ his neck.
She said to her dad, "See how (6) _nice_ he is?"

Dad began to pet the dog as he said, "OK, June. He can be
our pet. Choose a (7) _name_ for him."

June smiled and said, "We can call him Jake."

"Jake, let's get in the car," said Dad.

After they (8) _rode_ home, they had a great

(9) _time_ playing catch with Jake.

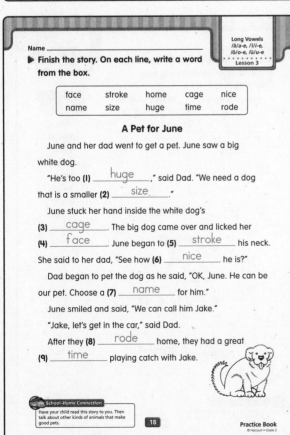

18

▶ Finish the story with words from the box.

different	ears	children
finally	short	hundred

A Dog Show Day

Pablo, Rose, and five other (1) _children_ went
to a dog show. They saw lots of (2) _different_
dogs. There were black dogs, tan dogs, gray dogs, and white
dogs. Some dogs had long tails. Other dogs had

(3) _short_ tails.

"There must be a (4) _hundred_ dogs here!"
said Rose.

"I like the dog that's in the ring now," Pablo said. "It's
got long, floppy (5) _ears_."

When the show was (6) _finally_
over, the dog that Pablo liked was the winner!

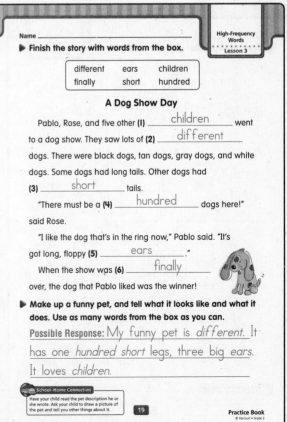

▶ Make up a funny pet, and tell what it looks like and what it
does. Use as many words from the box as you can.

Possible Response: My funny pet is *different*. It
has one *hundred short* legs, three big *ears*.
It loves *children*.

19

Name _____

▶ Below each sentence are three syllables.
Put two together to make a word that fits.
Write it on the line.

1. Gil plays the ___trombone___
   bone   trom   page

2. These are nice ___pancakes___.
   pan   tones   cakes

3. Jin made a ___mistake___.
   take   place   mis

4. Do you like my ___costume___?
   cos   cape   tume

5. This cake is ___homemade___.
   bake   home   made

6. The cat ran ___inside___.
   side   in   vite

7. We can ___locate___ our home.
   lo   cate   pose

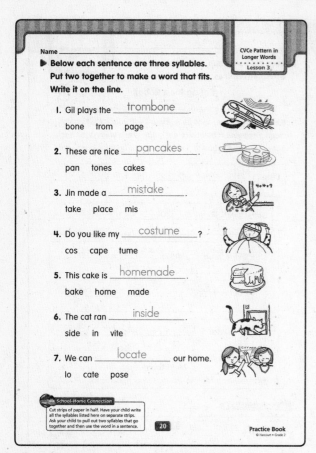

20

Name _____

▶ Read each sentence. If it is a statement, write *statement*.
If it is a question, write *question*.
If it is a command, write *command*.
If it an exclamation, write *exclamation*.

1. Get your backpacks. ___command___

2. It is time to go to school. ___statement___

3. Oh, the bus is coming! ___exclamation___

4. Do you want to be late? ___question___

5. Pick up your lunch box. ___command___

▶ Write each sentence correctly.

6. please water the plants

   Please water the plants.

7. look at the huge flower on my plant

   Look at the huge flower on my plant!

21

Name _____

▶ Circle the word that goes with each picture.

1. meal / male / met

2. leaf / left / feel

3. sale / sell / seal

4. shade / shed / sheep

5. felt / flea / feet

6. gave / geese / greets

7. pass / peas / pace

8. tea / eat / at

9. seat / sent / seed

10. jams / jeans / jeeps

11. clean / mean / keep

12. deed / deep / dream

22

Name _____

▶ Read the Spelling Words. Sort the words and write them where they belong.
Order may vary.

Words with *ee*	Words with *ea*
see	please
need	deal
sleep	mean
green	clean
keep	eat

Spelling Words

see
please
need
deal
sleep
mean
green
clean
keep
eat

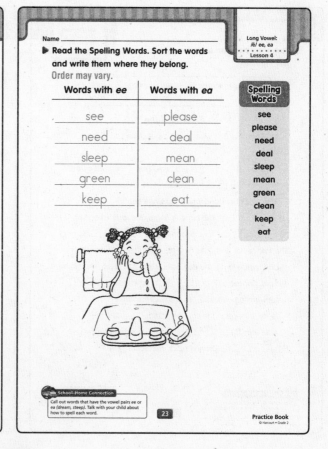

23

© Harcourt • Grade 2

8

Student Edition pp. 20–23

▶ Read the first paragraph. Fill in the chart.
Then read the next paragraph and write
the main idea.

Hamster Care

Remember to take good care of your hamster. Always handle
your hamster gently. If it is asleep, do not wake it. Make sure it
has fresh water and special hamster food. Take good care of
your hamster and it will live a happy life.

Detail	Detail	Detail
1. Handle it gently.	2. Do not wake it when it is sleeping.	3. Give it water and special food.

Main idea
Take good care of your hamster.

Hamster Workouts

A pet hamster needs to be active. Put a cardboard tube in
the cage so that the hamster can dash through it. A hamster
likes to run on an exercise wheel, too.

4. What is the main idea?
A pet hamster needs to be active.

24

▶ Circle and write the word that completes
each sentence.

1. My dog likes to ___sleep___ in my bed.
   (sleep) slap seas

2. A puppy nips with its ___teeth___.
   three (teeth) teens

3. I do not let my dog run into the ___street___.
   seed (street) steal

4. My dog will ___leap___ up for a ball.
   leak lamp (leap)

5. Dogs can swim at the ___beach___.
   beans bench (beach)

6. I fed a ___treat___ to my dog.
   tree (treat) tale

7. A dog is safe on its ___leash___.
   lash less (leash)

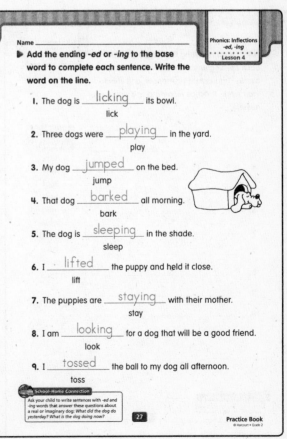

8. Dogs ___need___ to run and play.
   (need) net neat

25

▶ Write a word from the box that completes
each sentence.

sugar	bicycle	special	sometimes	exercise

1. A pet often needs ___special___ food.

2. Play catch with a dog so that it gets ___exercise___.

3. Some dogs can run as fast as a ___bicycle___.

4. My cat spilled a cup of white ___sugar___.

5. Her dog ___sometimes___ plays with other dogs.

▶ Write sentences that go with each picture. Use at least two
words from the box.

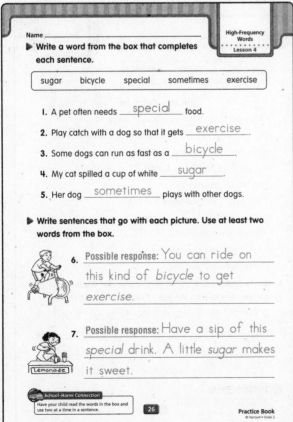

6. Possible response: You can ride on
this kind of *bicycle* to get
exercise.

7. Possible response: Have a sip of this
special drink. A little *sugar* makes
it sweet.

26

▶ Add the ending -ed or -ing to the base
word to complete each sentence. Write the
word on the line.

1. The dog is ___licking___ its bowl.
   lick

2. Three dogs were ___playing___ in the yard.
   play

3. My dog ___jumped___ on the bed.
   jump

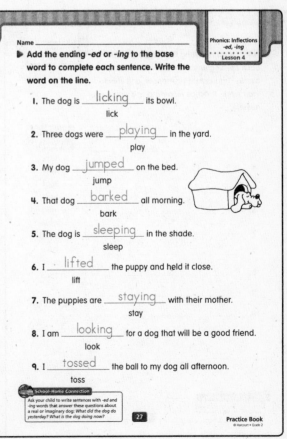

4. That dog ___barked___ all morning.
   bark

5. The dog is ___sleeping___ in the shade.
   sleep

6. I ___lifted___ the puppy and held it close.
   lift

7. The puppies are ___staying___ with their mother.
   stay

8. I am ___looking___ for a dog that will be a good friend.
   look

9. I ___tossed___ the ball to my dog all afternoon.
   toss

27

9

▶ Match each naming part with a telling part. Write a complete sentence.

Parts of a Sentence
Lesson 4

Naming Part	Telling Part
Butterflies	work hard.
Ants	make honey.
Spiders	fly.
Bees	make webs.

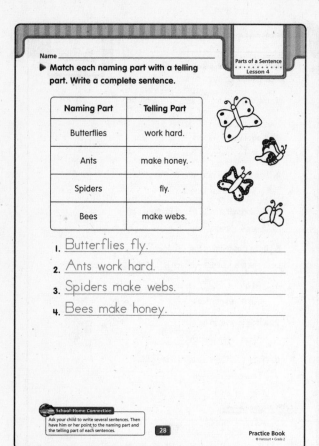

1. Butterflies fly.
2. Ants work hard.
3. Spiders make webs.
4. Bees make honey.

28

Practice Book
© Harcourt • Grade 2

Short Vowels
/a/a, /i/i;
CVC Pattern in
Longer Words
Lesson 5

▶ Circle the syllable that completes each word. Then write the syllable on the line.

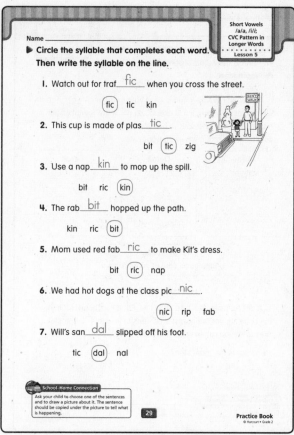

1. Watch out for traf __fic__ when you cross the street.
   (fic) tic kin

2. This cup is made of plas __tic__.
   bit (tic) zig

3. Use a nap __kin__ to mop up the spill.
   bit ric (kin)

4. The rab __bit__ hopped up the path.
   kin ric (bit)

5. Mom used red fab __ric__ to make Kit's dress.
   bit (ric) nap

6. We had hot dogs at the class pic __nic__.
   (nic) rip fab

7. Will's san __dal__ slipped off his foot.
   tic (dal) nal

29

Practice Book
© Harcourt • Grade 2

Theme 1
Review
Lesson 5

▶ Fold the paper along the dotted line. As each spelling word is read, write it in the blank. Then unfold your paper, and check your work. Practice respelling any words you missed.

1. _____
2. _____
3. _____
4. _____
5. _____
6. _____
7. _____
8. _____
9. _____
10. _____

Spelling Words

has
win
spot
best
mud
same
broke
rule
clean
sleep

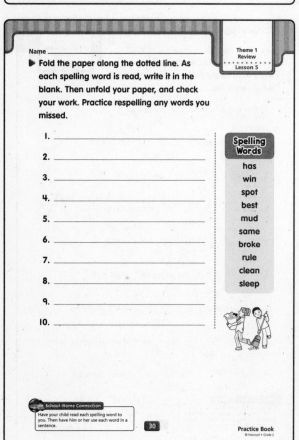

30

Practice Book
© Harcourt • Grade 2

High-Frequency
Words
Lesson 5

▶ Finish the story using words from the box.

sign	guess	different
bicycle	hundred	

The Jelly Bean Jar

Manny and his sister Tina looked at the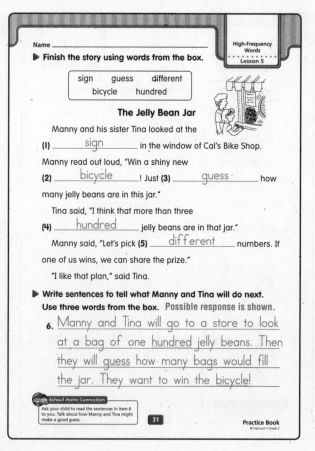

(1) ____sign____ in the window of Cal's Bike Shop.

Manny read out loud, "Win a shiny new

(2) ____bicycle____! Just (3) ____guess____ how

many jelly beans are in this jar."

Tina said, "I think that more than three

(4) ____hundred____ jelly beans are in that jar."

Manny said, "Let's pick (5) ____different____ numbers. If

one of us wins, we can share the prize."

"I like that plan," said Tina.

▶ Write sentences to tell what Manny and Tina will do next. Use three words from the box. **Possible response is shown.**

6. Manny and Tina will go to a store to look
   at a bag of one hundred jelly beans. Then
   they will guess how many bags would fill
   the jar. They want to win the bicycle!

31

Practice Book
© Harcourt • Grade 2

© Harcourt • Grade 2

Student Edition pp. 28–31

Name _____

▶ Add the **-s** or **-es** ending to the base word to make a word that completes the sentence. Write the word on the line.

1. Hand me those ___glasses___ **glass**

2. Rex walked nine ___blocks___ to the store. **block**

3. Marcus picked up ___shells___ at the beach. **shell**

4. Three ___foxes___ ran up the path. **fox**

5. This store sells everything for ___pets___ **pet**

6. The ___ducks___ in the pond were quacking. **duck**

7. All the girls wore green ___dresses___. **dress**

8. Mom packed six ___lunches___ **lunch**

9. The ___chairs___ were pushed under the table. **chair**

10. The ___boxes___ were taped closed. **box**

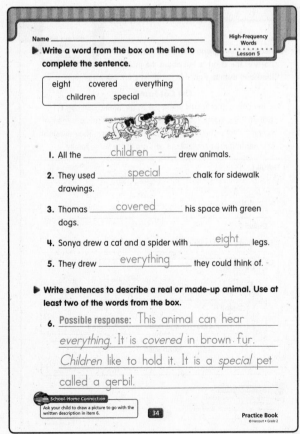

32

Name _____

▶ Read the story. Then complete the sentences in the chart to show how the two characters are alike and how they are different.

Goose's Shoes

Goose walked slowly. With each step, she yelped, "Ouch!" Her friend Hen came over. Goose yelled, "These new shoes hurt my feet! Ouch! I hate these new shoes!"

Hen looked at the shoes. Then she said softly, "I can help you, Goose. Your shoes are on the wrong feet." Hen helped Goose switch the left shoe with the right shoe.

"That feels much better," said Goose after she took a few steps. "Thanks, Hen." **Possible responses are shown.**

Goose	Hen	Goose and Hen
1. In the beginning Goose feels ___angry___	3. In the beginning, Hen feels ___sorry for___ ___her friend___	5. They are ___friends___
2. Goose tries to solve her problem by ___yelling___	4. Hen tries to solve the problem by ___thinking___	6. They both want ___Goose's___ ___shoes not___ ___to hurt her___

33

Name _____

▶ Write a word from the box on the line to complete the sentence.

eight	covered	everything
children	special	

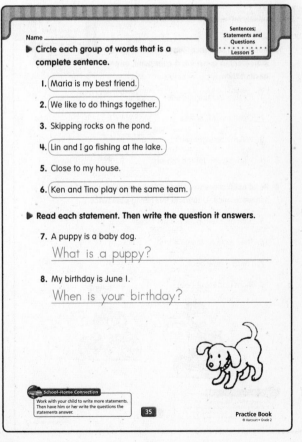

1. All the ___children___ drew animals.

2. They used ___special___ chalk for sidewalk drawings.

3. Thomas ___covered___ his space with green dogs.

4. Sonya drew a cat and a spider with ___eight___ legs.

5. They drew ___everything___ they could think of.

▶ Write sentences to describe a real or made-up animal. Use at least two of the words from the box.

6. _Possible response:_ This animal can hear _everything._ It is _covered_ in brown fur. _Children_ like to hold it. It is a _special_ pet called a gerbil.

34

Name _____

▶ Circle each group of words that is a complete sentence.

1. (Maria is my best friend.)

2. (We like to do things together.)

3. Skipping rocks on the pond.

4. (Lin and I go fishing at the lake.)

5. Close to my house.

6. (Ken and Tino play on the same team.)

▶ Read each statement. Then write the question it answers.

7. A puppy is a baby dog.
   What is a puppy?

8. My birthday is June 1.
   When is your birthday?

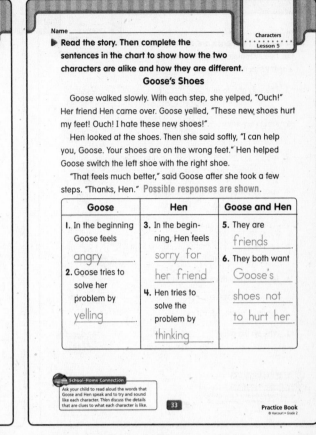

35

Long Vowels
/ā/a-e, /ī/i-e, /ō/
o-e, /(y)ōō/u-e;
CVCe Pattern in
Longer Words
Lesson 5

Name _____

▶ Below each sentence are three syllables.
Put two syllables together to make the correct
word. Write it on the line.

1. The dog got up at _____ sunrise _____.
   rise   sun   nick

2. Kim is my new _____ classmate _____
   name   class   mate

3. Al's _____ bedtime _____ is nine o'clock.
   time   side   bed

4. Luke jots down his homework in his
   _____ notebook _____
   place   book   note

5. Eve ate _____ pancakes _____ with jam.
   pan   dish   cakes

6. Max can play the trumpet and the
   _____ trombone _____
   bone   trom   drum

7. Who let the mice _____ escape _____?
   es   close   cape

School-Home Connection
Have your child read and then write each
word he or she made on a separate slip of
paper. Help your child cut each word into two
syllables. Then have your child put the words
back together.

36

Practice Book
© Harcourt • Grade 2

Long Vowel
/ē/ee, ea;
Inflections -ed, -ing
Lesson 5

Name _____

▶ Add the ending -ed or -ing to the base
word to complete the sentence. Write the
word on the line.

1. The cat is _____ sleeping _____ on the bench.   **sleep**

2. Mack _____ cleaned _____ up the den.   **clean**

3. Ada was _____ beating _____ eggs to make
   a cake.   **beat**

4. Dean is _____ meeting _____ his pal Greg at five.
   meet

5. The dog swam until it _____ reached _____ the shore.
   reach

6. The jaybird in the tree kept _____ screeching _____ at us
   until we left.   **screech**

7. Tea _____ leaked _____ out of the cracked cup.
   leak

8. The chicks were _____ peeping _____ as they ran up to
   the mother hen.   **peep**

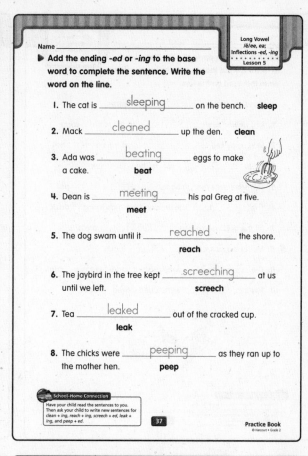

School-Home Connection
Have your child read the sentences to you.
Then ask your child to write new sentences for
clean + ing, reach + ing, screech + ed, leak +
ing, and peep + ed.

37

Practice Book
© Harcourt • Grade 2

Name _____

▶ Read each sentence. Write whether it is a
statement, a *question*, a *command*, or an
exclamation.

1. It's pouring rain outside! _____ exclamation _____

2. Close the windows. _____ command _____

3. Will my bike get wet? _____ question _____

4. Rain is good for the flowers. _____ statement _____

▶ Read each sentence. Underline the naming part of each
sentence once. Underline the telling part twice.

5. Sam and Ann bought new bikes.

6. They rode on the bike trail.

7. I read a new book.

8. Mom and I love books.

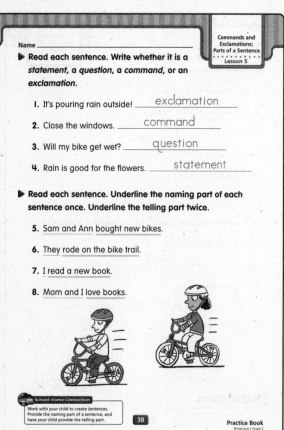

School-Home Connection
Work with your child to create sentences.
Provide the naming part of a sentence, and
have your child provide the telling part.

38

Practice Book
© Harcourt • Grade 2

Name _____

▶ Read the paragraph. Fill in the missing
parts of the chart to tell about the main
idea and details. Possible responses are shown.

The Cat Family

Pet cats and wild cats are in the same family. Wild cats
include lions, tigers, leopards, and bobcats. All cats are meat-
eating hunters. They have sharp teeth and claws. Their eyesight
and hearing are excellent. All cats are in the same family.

Detail 1
Wild cats include lions, tigers, leopards, and
bobcats.

Detail 2
2. All are meat-eating hunters.

Detail 3
3. They have sharp teeth and claws.

Detail 4
4. Their eyesight and hearing are excellent.

Main idea
Pet cats and wild cats are in the same family.

School-Home Connection
Have your child look at the paragraph and
write another detail that could fit in it. Then
have your child redraw the chart, adding the
new detail.

39

Practice Book
© Harcourt • Grade 2

Student Edition pp. 36–39

Page 40

Name _____

▶ Circle the word that goes with each picture.

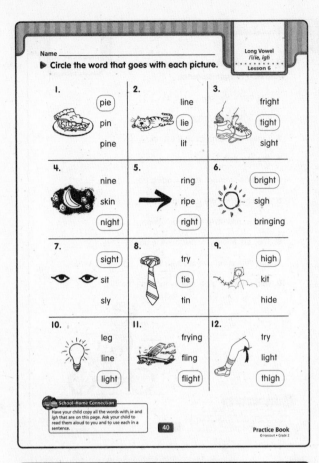

1. (pie) pin pine	2. line (lie) lit	3. fright (tight) sight
4. nine skin (night)	5. ring ripe (right)	6. (bright) sigh bringing
7. (sight) sit sly	8. try (tie) tin	9. (high) kit hide
10. leg line (light)	11. frying fling (flight)	12. try light (thigh)

School-Home Connection
Have your child copy all the words with *ie* and *igh* that are on this page. Ask your child to read them aloud to you and to use each in a sentence.

40

Practice Book
© Harcourt • Grade 2

Page 41

Name _____

▶ Read the Spelling Words. Sort the words and write them where they belong.

Order may vary.

Words with *ie*

1. _pie_
2. _tie_
3. _lie_

Words with *igh*

4. _high_
5. _light_
6. _night_
7. _bright_
8. _right_
9. _might_
10. _tight_

Spelling Words

pie
high
tie
light
lie
night
bright
right
might
tight

School-Home Connection
With your child, brainstorm and list words you know, in addition to the Spelling Words, that include the letters *ie* or *igh*. Discuss the spelling of each word.

41

Practice Book
© Harcourt • Grade 2

Page 42

Name _____

▶ Read the story. Complete the sentences in the chart to make two predictions.

Mom's Birthday Cake

"It's Mom's birthday today!" said Lucas. "Let's bake Mom a cake!"

"Good idea, Lucas! I will go and find a recipe," said Gina.

Lucas did not wait for the recipe. Instead, he got out some flour. Then he got out some salt. He got a cup of water, and two eggs. He mixed everything together.

Gina came back with the recipe.

"Oh, no Lucas!" she said. "What did you do?"

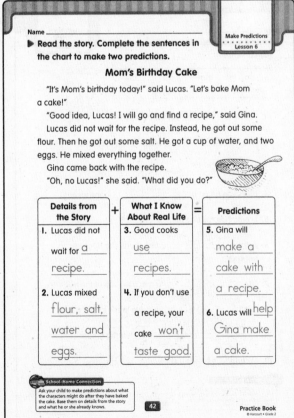

Details from the Story	+	What I Know About Real Life	=	Predictions
1. Lucas did not wait for a recipe.		3. Good cooks use recipes.		5. Gina will make a cake with a recipe.
2. Lucas mixed flour, salt, water and eggs.		4. If you don't use a recipe, your cake won't taste good.		6. Lucas will help Gina make a cake.

School-Home Connection
Ask your child to make predictions about what the characters might do after they have baked the cake. Base them on details from the story and what he or she already knows.

42

Practice Book
© Harcourt • Grade 2

Page 43

Name _____

▶ Circle the word in each sentence that has the *long i* vowel sound. Write it on the line.

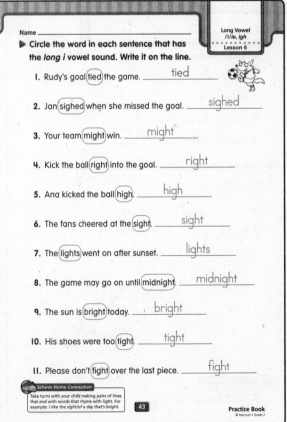

1. Rudy's goal (tied) the game. _tied_

2. Jan (sighed) when she missed the goal. _sighed_

3. Your team (might) win. _might_

4. Kick the ball (right) into the goal. _right_

5. Ana kicked the ball (high). _high_

6. The fans cheered at the (sight). _sight_

7. The (lights) went on after sunset. _lights_

8. The game may go on until (midnight). _midnight_

9. The sun is (bright) today. _bright_

10. His shoes were too (tight). _tight_

11. Please don't (fight) over the last piece. _fight_

School-Home Connection
Take turns with your child making pairs of lines that end with words that rhyme with *light*. For example: *I like the sight/of a day that's bright.*

43

Practice Book
© Harcourt • Grade 2

13

Student Edition pp. 40–43

© Harcourt • Grade 2

High-Frequency Words
Lesson 6

▶ Write the word from the box that completes the sentence.

brother	learn	caught
cheer	straight	lose

1. My _____brother_____ Dwight was teaching me to pitch.

2. I wanted to _____learn_____ how to throw a fastball.

3. Dwight threw the ball _____straight_____ to me.

4. I _____caught_____ the ball in my mitt.

5. Dwight jumped up to _____cheer_____ when I threw it back.

6. Dwight says good pitchers don't _____lose_____ many games.

▶ Use two words from the box to write a sentence that goes with each picture. **Possible responses are shown.**

7. _We cheer when the ball is caught._

8. _My brother and I learn to kick the ball._

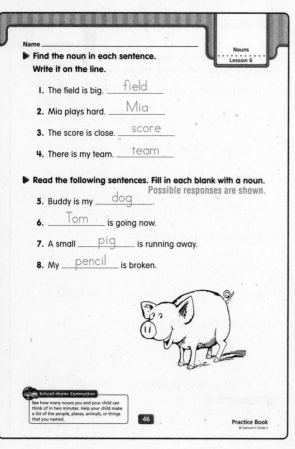

School-Home Connection
Have your child read the words in the box and use two at a time in a sentence.

44

Practice Book
© Harcourt • Grade 2

Inflections -ed, -ing
Lesson 6

▶ Write the base word of the underlined word next to each sentence.

1. The sun is shining. _____shine_____

2. Kim is riding her bike. _____ride_____

3. Carlos and Jo raced on the track. _____race_____

4. The friends hiked up a hill. _____hike_____

5. Children splashed in the wading pool. _____wade_____

6. Five children were using the slide. _____use_____

7. All the children liked being outside. _____like_____

8. They are hoping for another fine day. _____hope_____

9. She shared her crayons with Susan. _____share_____

10. Lela was saving her money for three months. _____save_____

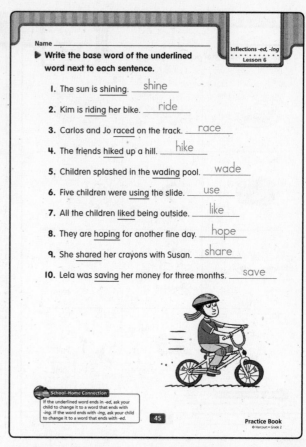

School-Home Connection
If the underlined word ends in -ed, ask your child to change it to a word that ends with -ing. If the word ends with -ing, ask your child to change it to a word that ends with -ed.

45

Practice Book
© Harcourt • Grade 2

Nouns
Lesson 6

▶ Find the noun in each sentence. Write it on the line.

1. The field is big. _____field_____

2. Mia plays hard. _____Mia_____

3. The score is close. _____score_____

4. There is my team. _____team_____

▶ Read the following sentences. Fill in each blank with a noun.
Possible responses are shown.

5. Buddy is my _____dog_____.

6. _____Tom_____ is going now.

7. A small _____pig_____ is running away.

8. My _____pencil_____ is broken.

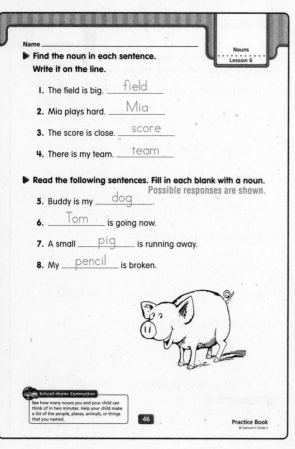

School-Home Connection
See how many nouns you and your child can think of in two minutes. Help your child make a list of the people, places, animals, or things that you named.

46

Practice Book
© Harcourt • Grade 2

Long Vowel /ā/ai, ay
Lesson 7

▶ Write the word from the box that completes the sentence.

day	gray	aim	trail
training	braid	paint	stay

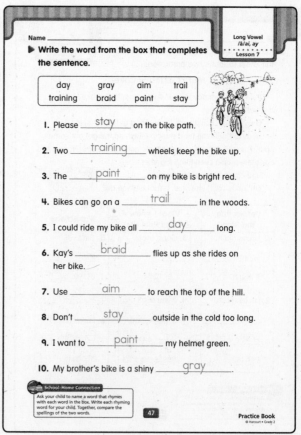

1. Please _____stay_____ on the bike path.

2. Two _____training_____ wheels keep the bike up.

3. The _____paint_____ on my bike is bright red.

4. Bikes can go on a _____trail_____ in the woods.

5. I could ride my bike all _____day_____ long.

6. Kay's _____braid_____ flies up as she rides on her bike.

7. Use _____aim_____ to reach the top of the hill.

8. Don't _____stay_____ outside in the cold too long.

9. I want to _____paint_____ my helmet green.

10. My brother's bike is a shiny _____gray_____.

School-Home Connection
Ask your child to name a word that rhymes with each word in the box. Write each rhyming word for your child. Together, compare the spellings of the two words.

47

Practice Book
© Harcourt • Grade 2

Student Edition pp. 44–47

Name _____

▶ Make two sets of cards for the Spelling Words. Lay them down and read them.
1. Put the words with *ai* in one group.
2. Put the words with *ay* in one group.

Spelling Words

pay
mail
paint
day
rain
stay
sail
way
train
tray

Words with *ai*	Words with *ay*
mail	pay
paint	day
rain	stay
sail	way
train	tray

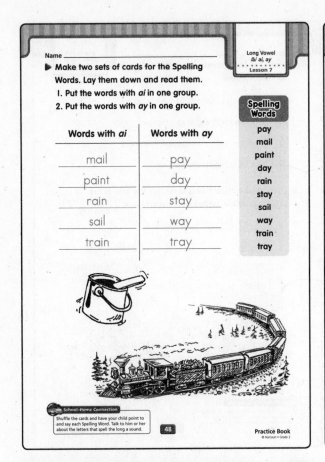

School–Home Connection
Shuffle the cards and have your child point to and say each Spelling Word. Talk to him or her about the letters that spell the long a sound.

48

Practice Book
© Harcourt • Grade 2

Name _____

▶ Read the story. Complete the sentences to fill out the chart and make two predictions.

The Slide

Tomás sat at the top of the slide. Papi stood at the bottom in the pool.

"Come on, Tomás," said Papi. "You can do it."

"Okay," said Tomás. "What if the water is over my head?"

"I will catch you!" said Papi. "Don't worry."

Tomás looked way down at his smiling father. He was not so sure. *What if Papi drops me?* he thought. Then he took a big breath. He pinched his nose with his fingers.

Details from the Story	+	What I Know About Real Life	=	Predictions
1. Papi tells Tomás he will catch him.		3. Fathers are good at helping their children.		5. Tomás will go down the slide.
2. Tomás took a big breath and pinched his nose.		4. You pinch your nose when you jump into water.		6. Papi will catch Tomás.

School–Home Connection
Encourage your child to give explanations for his or her predictions.

49

Practice Book
© Harcourt • Grade 2

Name _____

▶ Circle and write the word that completes each sentence.

1. Stack the dishes on the _____tray_____.
   train (tray) try

2. The breeze helped the boat _____sail_____ along.
   say (sail) seal

3. Keep trying, and you will not _____fail_____.
   file (fail) fill

4. Read to find the _____main_____ idea.
   (main) mine man

5. Do you know the _____way_____ home?
   why (way) waist

6. Humpty felt _____pain_____ when he fell.
   pan pay (pain)

7. Please _____wait_____ for me to catch up.
   way wade (wait)

8. Use your _____brain_____ to think.
   bran (brain) bring

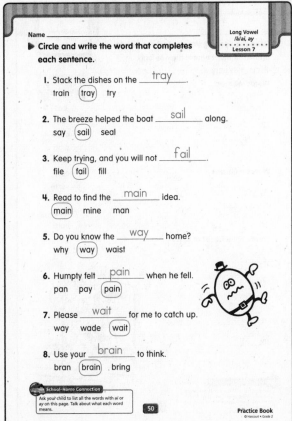

School–Home Connection
Ask your child to list all the words with ai or ay on this page. Talk about what each word means.

50

Practice Book
© Harcourt • Grade 2

Name _____

▶ Write the word from the box that completes the sentence.

coming	knee	idea	laughed
million	curve	world	

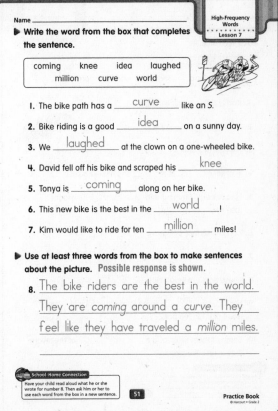

1. The bike path has a _____curve_____ like an *S*.

2. Bike riding is a good _____idea_____ on a sunny day.

3. We _____laughed_____ at the clown on a one-wheeled bike.

4. David fell off his bike and scraped his _____knee_____.

5. Tonya is _____coming_____ along on her bike.

6. This new bike is the best in the _____world_____!

7. Kim would like to ride for ten _____million_____ miles!

▶ Use at least three words from the box to make sentences about the picture. Possible response is shown.

8. The bike riders are the best in the world. They are *coming* around a *curve*. They feel like they have traveled a *million* miles.

School–Home Connection
Have your child read aloud what he or she wrote for number 8. Then ask him or her to use each word from the box in a new sentence.

51

Practice Book
© Harcourt • Grade 2

Student Edition pp. 48–51

▶ Write the two words that make up each underlined compound word.

1. The bikes are in the driveway. __drive__ __way__

2. The mailbox is filled with letters. __mail__ __box__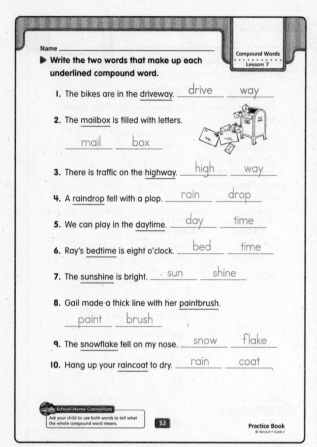

3. There is traffic on the highway. __high__ __way__

4. A raindrop fell with a plop. __rain__ __drop__

5. We can play in the daytime. __day__ __time__

6. Ray's bedtime is eight o'clock. __bed__ __time__

7. The sunshine is bright. __sun__ __shine__

8. Gail made a thick line with her paintbrush. __paint__ __brush__

9. The snowflake fell on my nose. __snow__ __flake__

10. Hang up your raincoat to dry. __rain__ __coat__

School-Home Connection
Ask your child to use both words to tell what the whole compound word means.

52

▶ Underline each plural noun in the sentences below.

1. The children will plant tulips in the garden.

2. The adults are going to plant roses.

3. The garden will have many pretty flowers.

4. I think we should plant trees too.

▶ Think of new plural nouns to replace the ones in the sentences above. Write each new sentence. Possible responses are shown.

5. The ladies will plant daisies in the garden.

6. The men are going to plant trees.

7. The garden will have many quiet ponds.

8. I think we should plant bushes, too.

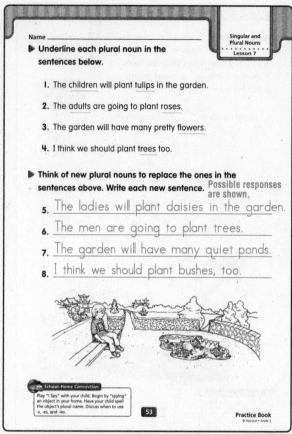

School-Home Connection
Play "I Spy" with your child. Begin by "spying" an object in your home. Have your child spell the object's plural name. Discuss when to use -s, -es, and -ies.

53

▶ Write a word from the box to complete each sentence.

| star | harm | starts | part | darting |
| sharp | yard | march | dark | large |

1. Karl is sitting outside in his __yard__

2. It is night, and the sky is __dark__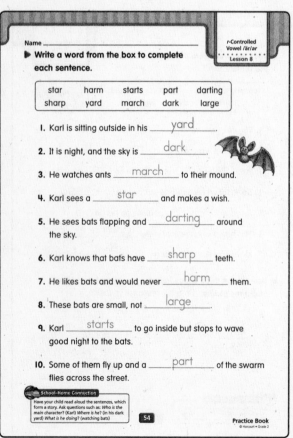

3. He watches ants __march__ to their mound.

4. Karl sees a __star__ and makes a wish.

5. He sees bats flapping and __darting__ around the sky.

6. Karl knows that bats have __sharp__ teeth.

7. He likes bats and would never __harm__ them.

8. These bats are small, not __large__.

9. Karl __starts__ to go inside but stops to wave good night to the bats.

10. Some of them fly up and a __part__ of the swarm flies across the street.

School-Home Connection
Have your child read aloud the sentences, which form a story. Ask questions such as: Who is the main character? (Karl) Where is he? (in his dark yard) What is he doing? (watching bats)

54

▶ Read the Spelling Words. Sort the words and write them where they belong.
Order may vary.

Words with art

1. __art__

2. __start__

3. __part__

Words with arn

4. __barn__

5. __yarn__

Words without art or arn

6. __car__

7. __farm__

8. __card__

9. __dark__

10. __hard__

Spelling Words

car
art
barn
start
farm
card
yarn
part
dark
hard

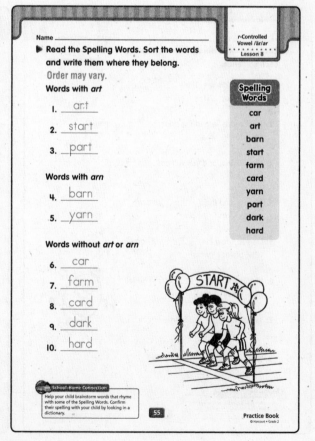

School-Home Connection
Help your child brainstorm words that rhyme with some of the Spelling Words. Confirm their spelling with your child by looking in a dictionary.

55

▶ Read the story. Complete the sentences in the chart to show the plot.

How Leopard Got His Spots

Long ago, Leopard had no spots. When he tried to hunt, the other animals could see him. They ran away. Leopard did not have food to eat.

"Who can help me?" Leopard asked.

"I will help you, Leopard," said a boy. "Be still!" The boy put his paintbrush in black paint. He covered Leopard with spots. The spots helped Leopard hide.

Now Leopard can hunt and eat.

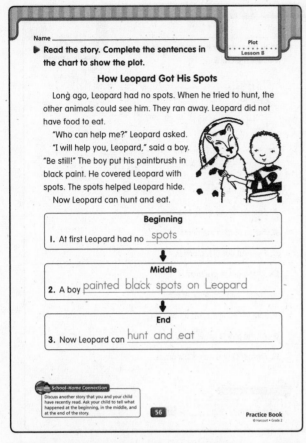

Beginning

1. At first Leopard had no _spots_

Middle

2. A boy _painted black spots on Leopard_

End

3. Now Leopard can _hunt and eat_

56

▶ Finish the story. On each line, write a word from the box.

| card | large | dart | harm | dark | star |

BATS!

When the sky gets (1) _dark_, bats wake up. They dash

and (2) _dart_ around in the air. Bats may seem scary,

but most will never (3) _harm_ you. Most bats are small

animals, but the flying fox is a (4) _large_ bat. Its wings

are five feet across!

▶ Circle and write the word that completes the sentence.

5. A cat has _sharp_ teeth.
   share shape (sharp)

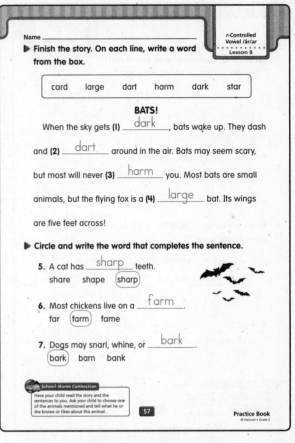

6. Most chickens live on a _farm_
   far (farm) fame

7. Dogs may snarl, whine, or _bark_
   (bark) barn bank

57

▶ Complete the sentences with words from the box.

| fair | half | though | ago | clear | accept |

1. Long _ago_, Rabbit wanted to race Turtle.

2. It was _clear_ that Rabbit was much faster.

3. "I _accept_ your offer," said Turtle.

4. When the race was _half_ over, Rabbit was ahead.

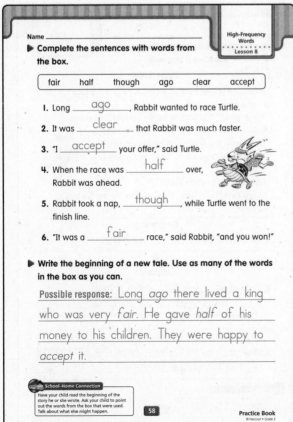

5. Rabbit took a nap, _though_, while Turtle went to the finish line.

6. "It was a _fair_ race," said Rabbit, "and you won!"

▶ Write the beginning of a new tale. Use as many of the words in the box as you can.

Possible response: Long *ago* there lived a king who was very *fair*. He gave *half* of his money to his children. They were happy to *accept* it.

58

▶ Below each sentence are three syllables. Put two together to make a word that fits. Write it on the line.

1. The stars _sparkle_ in the sky.
   kle spar ring

2. It was dark, so Mom lit a _candle_
   can bun dle

3. Iris found a black _marble_
   jum ble mar

4. The dart hit right in the _middle_
   dle mid sad

5. Mark ate an _apple_ for a snack.
   ple sim ap

6. David blows a large _bubble_
   bub ble thim

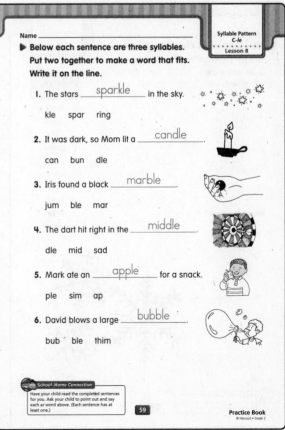

59

Page 60

Name _____

Proper Nouns
Lesson 8

▶ **Read each group of words below. If the words are proper nouns, write *proper noun*. If they are not proper nouns, write *no*.**

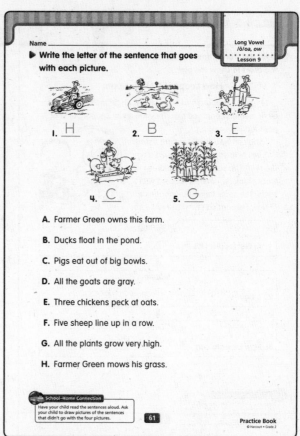

1. Mr. Tibbs ___proper noun___
2. Elm Street ___proper noun___
3. pretty birds ___no___
4. Stacey ___proper noun___
5. Heritage Elementary School ___proper noun___
6. my friend ___no___

▶ **Write each sentence correctly. Begin each proper noun with a capital letter.**

7. bessie took her pet snake, buddy, to show and tell.

Bessie took her pet snake, Buddy, to show and tell.

8. My pet bird, tiny, can say five words.

My pet bird, Tiny, can say five words.

School-Home Connection
Write down the names and occupations of people in your family or people you know. Ask your child to point out the proper nouns that should be capitalized.

60

Practice Book
© Harcourt • Grade 2

Page 61

Name _____

Long Vowel
/ō/oa, ow
Lesson 9

▶ **Write the letter of the sentence that goes with each picture.**

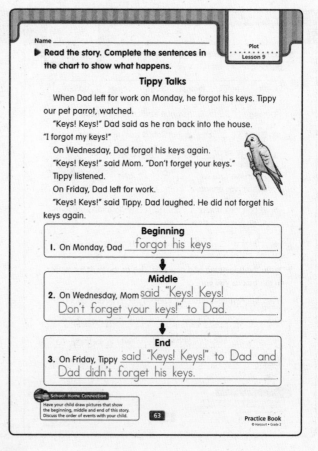

1. H   2. B   3. E
4. C   5. G

A. Farmer Green owns this farm.

B. Ducks float in the pond.

C. Pigs eat out of big bowls.

D. All the goats are gray.

E. Three chickens peck at oats.

F. Five sheep line up in a row.

G. All the plants grow very high.

H. Farmer Green mows his grass.

School-Home Connection
Have your child read the sentences aloud. Ask your child to draw pictures of the sentences that didn't go with the four pictures.

61

Practice Book
© Harcourt • Grade 2

Page 62

Name _____

Long Vowel /ō/
oa, ow
Lesson 9

▶ **Read the Spelling Words. Sort the words and write them where they belong.**

Order may vary.

Words with oa

1. boat
2. coat
3. float
4. load
5. soak

Words with ow

6. snow
7. grow
8. own
9. low
10. bowl

Spelling Words

boat
snow
coat
grow
float
own
low
load
soak
bowl

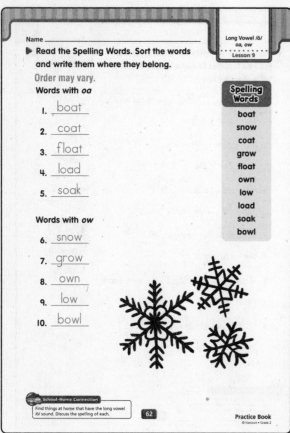

School-Home Connection
Find things at home that have the long vowel /ō/ sound. Discuss the spelling of each.

62

Practice Book
© Harcourt • Grade 2

Page 63

Name _____

Plot
Lesson 9

▶ **Read the story. Complete the sentences in the chart to show what happens.**

Tippy Talks

When Dad left for work on Monday, he forgot his keys. Tippy our pet parrot, watched.

"Keys! Keys!" Dad said as he ran back into the house. "I forgot my keys!"

On Wednesday, Dad forgot his keys again.

"Keys! Keys!" said Mom. "Don't forget your keys." Tippy listened.

On Friday, Dad left for work.

"Keys! Keys!" said Tippy. Dad laughed. He did not forget his keys again.

Beginning
1. On Monday, Dad forgot his keys

↓

Middle
2. On Wednesday, Mom said "Keys! Keys! Don't forget your keys!" to Dad.

↓

End
3. On Friday, Tippy said "Keys! Keys!" to Dad and Dad didn't forget his keys.

School-Home Connection
Have your child draw pictures that show the beginning, middle and end of this story. Discuss the order of events with your child.

63

Practice Book
© Harcourt • Grade 2

© Harcourt • Grade 2

Page 64

▶ **Circle and write the word that completes
the sentence.**

1. Edna lives on the ___coast___ by the sea.

   cost   (coast)   coat

2. She ___shows___ Dad a note to her friend, Jeb.

   (shows)   shuts   soles

3. She tells Jeb about Gus, her pet ___goat___

   (goat)   got   goal

4. Gus likes to eat jam on his ___toast___.

   tossed   tows   (toast)

5. Gus eats ice cream out of a ___bowl___

   boat   (bowl)   ball

6. That's why Gus has ___grown___ so big!

   grain   gone   (grown)

▶ **Write a sentence about Gus the goat. Use one of these
words: _float, slow, loaf,_ or _snow._** Possible response:

Gus the goat likes to play in the snow.

School–Home Connection
Have your child read the sentences to you.
Then work together to make up more silly
things that Gus the goat (who eats everything!)
might eat.

64

Practice Book
© Harcourt • Grade 2

Page 65

▶ **Complete the story with words from
the box.**

| believe | brought | impossible | enough |
| early | understand | quite | |

It Cannot Be!

The farmer got up (1) ___early___, before

sunrise. He (2) ___brought___ a basket with him. He

was going to collect eggs. When he checked the hens' nests, he

could not (3) ___believe___ it. The eggs were all gold!

"This is (4) ___impossible___!" he cried. "It cannot be!"

His hens were (5) ___quite___ upset with him.

"We don't (6) ___understand___ why you're not

happy," they said. "We do our best for you, but it's never good

(7) ___enough___. Don't you like gold eggs?"

"My hens can talk?" croaked the farmer. "Help!"

Then he woke up.

▶ **Write the answer to each clue on the line.**

8. This word means "all you need." ___enough___

9. This word is the opposite of late. ___early___

School–Home Connection
Have your child read the story to you. Then,
talk about it together. Ask your child questions
such as _What do you think he did after he
woke up?_

65

Practice Book
© Harcourt • Grade 2

Page 66

▶ **Write the two words that make up each
underlined compound word.**

1. The <u>snowflakes</u> fell softly. ___snow___ ___flakes___

2. A <u>rainbow</u> filled the sky. ___rain___ ___bow___

3. The <u>rowboat</u> is on the lake. ___row___ ___boat___

4. Yun-Hee ate hot <u>oatmeal</u>. ___oat___ ___meal___

5. My dad is a <u>grownup</u>. ___grown___ ___up___

6. Trains run on <u>railroad</u> tracks.

   ___rail___ ___road___

7. Let's drive to the <u>seacoast</u>. ___sea___ ___coast___

8. We drank tea from a <u>teacup</u>.

   ___tea___ ___cup___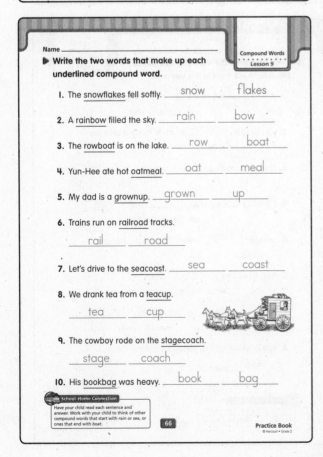

9. The cowboy rode on the <u>stagecoach</u>.

   ___stage___ ___coach___

10. His <u>bookbag</u> was heavy. ___book___ ___bag___

School–Home Connection
Have your child read each sentence and
answer. Work with your child to think of other
compound words that start with _rain_ or _sea,_ or
ones that end with _boat._

66

Practice Book
© Harcourt • Grade 2

Page 67

▶ **Look at the picture clue. Write the holiday
from the box that matches each clue.
Begin each proper noun with a capital letter.**

| groundhog day | valentine's day | mother's day |
| thanksgiving | presidents' day | veterans day |

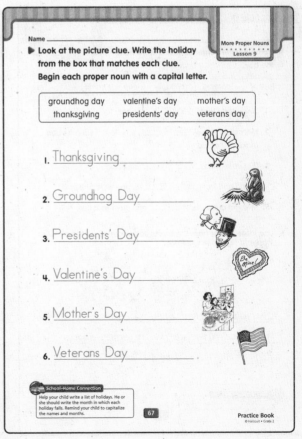

1. ___Thanksgiving___

2. ___Groundhog Day___

3. ___Presidents' Day___

4. ___Valentine's Day___

5. ___Mother's Day___

6. ___Veterans Day___

School–Home Connection
Help your child write a list of holidays. He or
she should write the month in which each
holiday falls. Remind your child to capitalize
the names and months.

67

Practice Book
© Harcourt • Grade 2

Name _____

▶ Circle and write the word that completes the sentence.

1. Toss the ball as ___high___ as you can.

   (high)   hide   sight

2. When our team lost, we all ___sighed___.

   singing   (sighed)   slight

3. Walk straight ahead, and then turn ___right___.

   ring   might   (right)

4. The ___sunlight___ is bright today.

   frighten   nightstand   (sunlight)

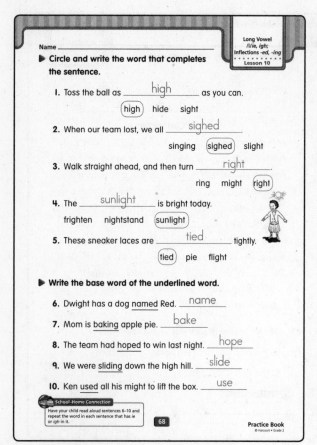

5. These sneaker laces are ___tied___ tightly.

   (tied)   pie   flight

▶ Write the base word of the underlined word.

6. Dwight has a dog named Red. ___name___

7. Mom is baking apple pie. ___bake___

8. The team had hoped to win last night. ___hope___

9. We were sliding down the high hill. ___slide___

10. Ken used all his might to lift the box. ___use___

68

Practice Book
© Harcourt • Grade 2

Name _____

▶ Fold the paper along the dotted line. As each Spelling Word is read, write it in the blank. Then unfold your paper, and check your work. Practice spelling any words you missed.

1. _____

2. _____

3. _____

4. _____

5. _____

6. _____

7. _____

8. _____

9. _____

10. _____

Spelling Words

tie
light
mail
day
barn
dark
hard
snow
soak
own

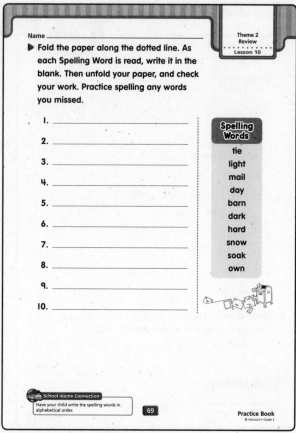

69

Practice Book
© Harcourt • Grade 2

Name _____

▶ Complete the sentence with a word from the box.

| half | coming | enough | idea | cheer |

1. Uncle Nate was ___coming___ to stay for a week.

2. Mom didn't have ___enough___ time to bake a cake and make dinner too.

3. "I have a good ___idea___," said Dad.

4. "Elena and I will do ___half___ the work," he said.

5. Mom let out a ___cheer___ and gave us a hug.

▶ Use three words from the box in sentences about the picture.
Possible response is shown.

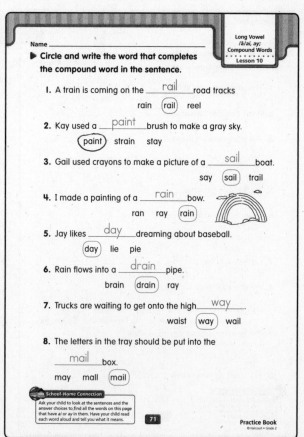

Everyone *cheered* when Mom came in with the cake. When we had all eaten *enough*, *half* of the cake was still left.

70

Practice Book
© Harcourt • Grade 2

Name _____

▶ Circle and write the word that completes the compound word in the sentence.

1. A train is coming on the ___rail___road tracks

   rain   (rail)   reel

2. Kay used a ___paint___brush to make a gray sky.

   (paint)   strain   stay

3. Gail used crayons to make a picture of a ___sail___boat.

   say   (sail)   trail

4. I made a painting of a ___rain___bow.

   ran   ray   (rain)

5. Jay likes ___day___dreaming about baseball.

   (day)   lie   pie

6. Rain flows into a ___drain___pipe.

   brain   (drain)   ray

7. Trucks are waiting to get onto the high___way___.

   waist   (way)   wail

8. The letters in the tray should be put into the ___mail___box.

   may   mall   (mail)

71

Practice Book
© Harcourt • Grade 2

Student Edition pp. 68–71

© Harcourt • Grade 2

▶ **Read the story. Fill out the chart to make two predictions.** Possible responses are shown.

Racing Down the Field

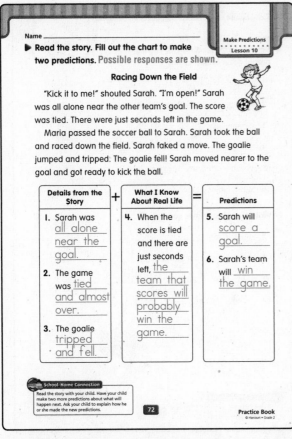

"Kick it to me!" shouted Sarah. "I'm open!" Sarah was all alone near the other team's goal. The score was tied. There were just seconds left in the game.

Maria passed the soccer ball to Sarah. Sarah took the ball and raced down the field. Sarah faked a move. The goalie jumped and tripped. The goalie fell! Sarah moved nearer to the goal and got ready to kick the ball.

Details from the Story	+	What I Know About Real Life	=	Predictions
1. Sarah was all alone near the goal.		4. When the score is tied and there are just seconds left, the team that scores will probably win the game.		5. Sarah will score a goal.
2. The game was tied and almost over.				6. Sarah's team will win the game.
3. The goalie tripped and fell.				

School-Home Connection
Read the story with your child. Have your child make two more predictions about what will happen next. Ask your child to explain how he or she made the new predictions.

72

Practice Book
© Harcourt • Grade 2

▶ **Complete the story with words from the box.**

| learn | world | believe | ago | brother |

Luke's Flute Lessons

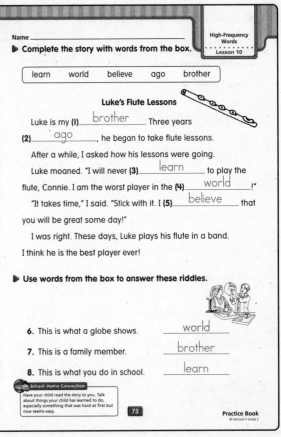

Luke is my **(1)** brother . Three years

(2) ago , he began to take flute lessons.

After a while, I asked how his lessons were going.

Luke moaned. "I will never **(3)** learn to play the

flute, Connie. I am the worst player in the **(4)** world !"

"It takes time," I said. "Stick with it. I **(5)** believe that

you will be great some day!"

I was right. These days, Luke plays his flute in a band.

I think he is the best player ever!

▶ **Use words from the box to answer these riddles.**

6. This is what a globe shows. _____ world

7. This is a family member. _____ brother

8. This is what you do in school. _____ learn

School-Home Connection
Have your child read the story to you. Talk about things your child has learned to do, especially something that was hard at first but now seems easy.

73

Practice Book
© Harcourt • Grade 2

▶ **Circle all the nouns in the sentences.**

1. George and Martha read a book.

2. Two boys were in a boat at a lake.

3. Their boat got stuck on the sand.

4. Water spilled into the boat.

5. The boys in the story decided to walk home.

▶ **Complete each sentence with a plural noun.**
Possible responses are shown.

6. I like to collect _____ coins

7. The cook bakes tasty _____ pies

8. My dad works with _____ tools

9. The house has many _____ windows

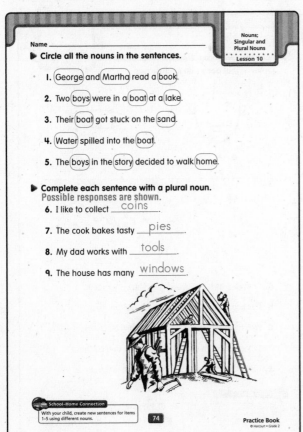

School-Home Connection
With your child, create new sentences for items 1–5 using different nouns.

74

Practice Book
© Harcourt • Grade 2

▶ **Finish the story by writing a word from the box on each line.**

| farmstand | arms | large |
| start | pardon | cars |

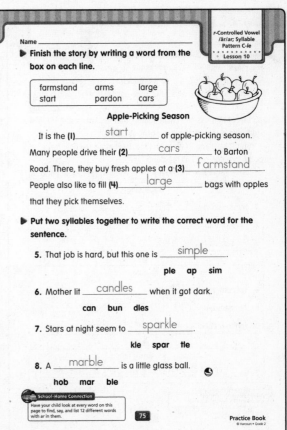

Apple-Picking Season

It is the **(1)** start of apple-picking season.

Many people drive their **(2)** cars to Barton

Road. There, they buy fresh apples at a **(3)** farmstand

People also like to fill **(4)** large bags with apples

that they pick themselves.

▶ **Put two syllables together to write the correct word for the sentence.**

5. That job is hard, but this one is _____ simple

    ple   ap   sim

6. Mother lit _____ candles when it got dark.

    can   bun   dles

7. Stars at night seem to _____ sparkle

    kle   spar   tle

8. A _____ marble is a little glass ball.

    hob   mar   ble

School-Home Connection
Have your child look at every word on this page to find, say, and list 12 different words with ar in them.

75

Practice Book
© Harcourt • Grade 2

© Harcourt • Grade 2

Long Vowel /ō/oa, ow; Compound Words
Lesson 10

▶ Write the two words that make up the underlined compound word.

1. A sailboat raced on the sea. ___sail___ ___boat___

2. Mom had a carload of kids. ___car___ ___load___

3. Lee throws snowballs. ___snow___ ___balls___

4. Uncle Ned is a grownup. ___grown___ ___up___

5. Joan puts on her raincoat. ___rain___ ___coat___

6. We ate meatloaf last night. ___meat___ ___loaf___

7. A showoff boasts and brags. ___show___ ___off___

8. Vin ate oatmeal and toast. ___oat___ ___meal___

9. Let's stop at that roadside stand to get snow peas. ___road___ ___side___

School-Home Connection
Help your child use the two words in *sailboat, carload, snowballs, raincoat, meatloaf,* and *roadside* to explain the meaning of each compound word.

76

Practice Book
© Harcourt • Grade 2

Proper Nouns
Lesson 10

▶ Read each group of words. Write the proper noun correctly.

1. saturday, weekend, day ___Saturday___

2. flag day, songs, celebrate ___Flag Day___

3. summer, july, hot ___July___

4. spring, rainy, march ___March___

5. weekday, thursday, afternoon ___Thursday___

6. picnic, holiday, labor day ___Labor Day___

▶ Write the place names correctly.

7. tampa, florida ___Tampa, Florida___

8. san diego, california ___San Diego, California___

9. dallas, texas ___Dallas, Texas___

10. chicago, illinois ___Chicago, Illinois___

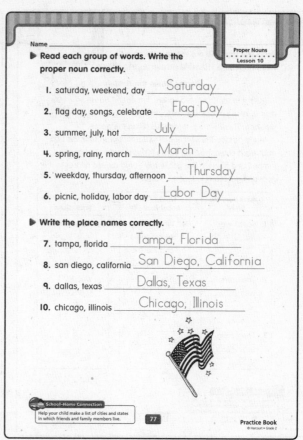

School-Home Connection
Help your child make a list of cities and states in which friends and family members live.

77

Practice Book
© Harcourt • Grade 2

Plot
Lesson 10

▶ Read the story. Complete the sentences in the chart. Possible responses are shown.

At the Beach

Yen put the last shell on her sand castle. "It's finished!" she said.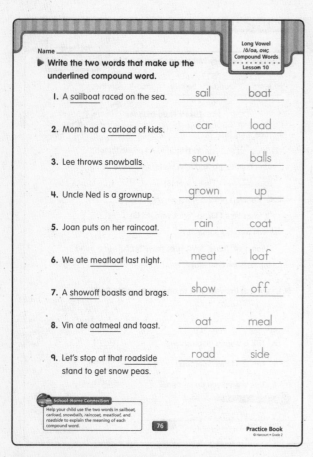

"I want to make the castle taller!" said her little sister, Vai. Vai started to dump sand on top of Yen's castle.

"Stop!" said Yen. "I have an idea. I will dig a big hole for a pond. You can help fill the pond."

"Okay!" said Vai, as she ran off to fetch water for the pond.

Beginning
1. Yen finished _her sandcastle_.
2. Vai wanted to _make Yen's castle taller_.
3. Vai started to _dump sand on Yen's castle_.

↓

Middle
4. Yen told Vai _to stop_.
5. Yen decided to _dig a hole for a pond_.
6. Yen told Vai she could help _fill the pond_.

↓

End
7. Vai _ran off to fetch water for the pond_.

School-Home Connection
Ask your child how the story would be different if Yen had gotten upset with her little sister. What would Yen say in the beginning, in the middle, and at the end?

78

Practice Book
© Harcourt • Grade 2

Digraphs /ch/ch, tch; /sh/sh; /th/th
Lesson 11

▶ Read the sentences. Write the letter of the sentence that goes with each picture.

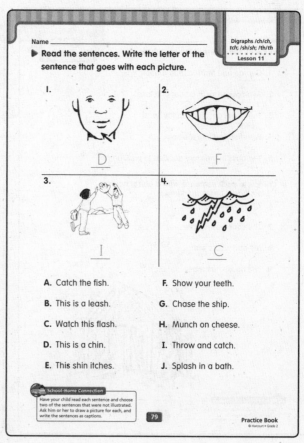

1. ___D___

2. ___F___

3. ___I___

4. ___C___

A. Catch the fish.

B. This is a leash.

C. Watch this flash.

D. This is a chin.

E. This shin itches.

F. Show your teeth.

G. Chase the ship.

H. Munch on cheese.

I. Throw and catch.

J. Splash in a bath.

School-Home Connection
Have your child read each sentence and choose two of the sentences that were not illustrated. Ask him or her to draw a picture for each, and write the sentences as captions.

79

Practice Book
© Harcourt • Grade 2

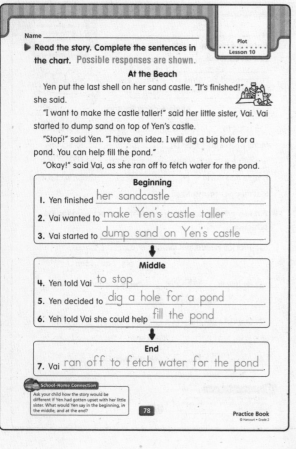

Name _____

▶ Read the Spelling Words. Sort the words and write them where they belong.
Order may vary.

Words with ch or tch

1. lunch
2. chop
3. catch
4. each
5. such

Words with sh

6. shape
7. wish
8. show

Words with th

9. then
10. bath

Spelling Words

lunch
shape
wish
chop
show
catch
then
each
bath
such

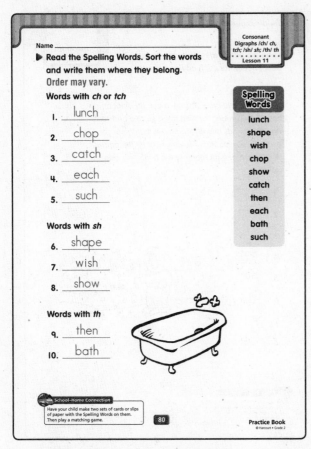

80

Practice Book
© Harcourt • Grade 2

Name _____

▶ Read the passage. Then answer the questions about the author's purpose.
Possible responses are shown.

A Puppy Named Noodle

"What shall we name our new puppy?" Dad asked Mai at dinner. Mai thought hard about a name. She did not notice her baby brother dropping noodles on the floor. Suddenly the puppy popped out from under a chair.

"Look, Mai!" said Dad. The puppy had a noodle stuck to his nose. "He's a poodle with a noodle!"

Mai giggled. "I think that's a good name," she said. "Let's call him Noodle!"

Type of Writing 1. a story

Author's Purpose 2. to tell a funny story

Clues 3. The puppy gets a noodle stuck to his nose.

4. Dad says "a poodle with a noodle."

5. Noodle is a funny name for a dog.

81

Practice Book
© Harcourt • Grade 2

Name _____

▶ Circle and write the word that completes each sentence.

1. Ms. Tharp is teaching the class about painting.
   (teaching)   hatching   thinking

2. Shane painted thin lines with a brush.
   (thin)   shin   chin

3. Cho's painting shows a tree with thick branches
   lashes   marches   (branches)

4. Thea made a painting of all kinds of shapes
   chase   (shapes)   fifth

5. Ruth mixed paints to get a reddish brown.
   switch   those   (reddish)

6. Archer painted a dish of peaches
   crushes   (peaches)   catches

7. Thad painted a shark with sharp teeth.
   (sharp)   thank   chart

8. Each child chose something to paint.
   those   (chose)   show

82

Practice Book
© Harcourt • Grade 2

Name _____

▶ Complete the story with words from the box.

draw	picture	question	minute
bought	worry	especially	sure

Charlie Paints

Grandma (1) bought an artist pad for Charlie.

She was (2) sure that Charlie would like it, and he did. Charlie loved to (3) draw and color. He (4) especially liked making cars. "What should I put in my (5) picture ?"

he asked Grandma.

"I think I know the answer to that

(6) question ," said Grandma with a smile. "In just a

(7) minute I'll see a car on the page."

Charlie went right to work. Then he held up his pad.

"See?" he said. "There is no need to (8) worry

that I only make cars."

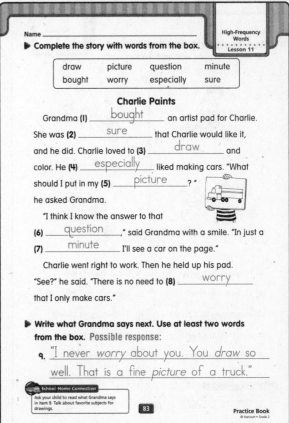

▶ Write what Grandma says next. Use at least two words from the box. Possible response:

9. "I never *worry* about you. You *draw* so well. That is a fine *picture* of a truck."

83

Practice Book
© Harcourt • Grade 2

Student Edition pp. 80–83

▶ **Put two syllables together to write a word that fits in the sentence.**

1. Shane looked out the back __window__ .
   dow   win   el

2. All of a __sudden__ , a little animal ran past.
   tist   den   sud

3. The animal was a striped __chipmunk__ .
   munk   shop   chip

4. The animal ran past a pile of __rubbish__ .
   sham   bish   rub

5. It dashed into the __garden__ .
   gar   shad   den

6. The animal started to __collect__ seeds.
   lect   ten   col

7. Shane got an artist pad and a __pencil__ .
   con   cil   pen

8. What do you __suppose__ Shane will sketch?
   pose   com   sup

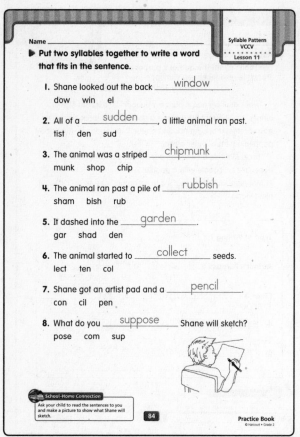

School-Home Connection
Ask your child to read the sentences to you and make a picture to show what Shane will sketch.

84

▶ **Read the paragraph. Write the correct abbreviation for each day and month.**

Fall

I love the fall. Every **(1)** September, **(2)** October, and **(3)** November, the weather is so nice and cool. On **(4)** Saturday and **(5)** Sunday my family spends a lot of time outdoors. We know that **(6)** December, **(7)** January, and **(8)** February will bring very cold weather.

1. Sept.
2. Oct.
3. Nov.
4. Sat.
5. Sun.
6. Dec.
7. Jan.
8. Feb.

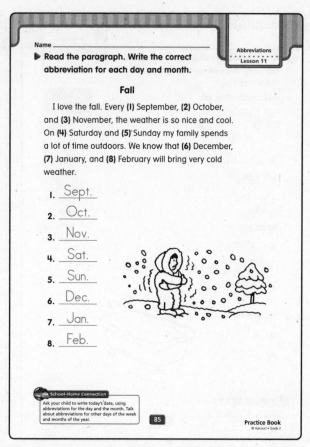

School-Home Connection
Ask your child to write today's date, using abbreviations for the day and the month. Talk about abbreviations for other days of the week and months of the year.

85

▶ **Read the sentences. Write the letter of the sentence that goes with each picture.**

1. F
2. A
3. G
4. H

A. Ladybugs are tiny.   F. This is very messy.

B. Make a silly face.   G. Monkeys are funny.

C. Pay money for candy.   H. It is hungry for honey.

D. Hug a fuzzy kitten.   I. It is a baby donkey.

E. The valley is grassy.   J. Each cherry is tasty.

School-Home Connection
Have your child read aloud all the sentences and draw or describe a picture that could go with each sentence that is not illustrated.

86

▶ **Read the Spelling Words. Sort the words and write them where they belong.**

Order may vary.

Words with _ey_

1. key
2. money

Words with _y_

3. very
4. messy
5. lady
6. happy
7. baby
8. funny
9. candy
10. sunny

Spelling Words

very
messy
lady
happy
key
baby
money
funny
candy
sunny

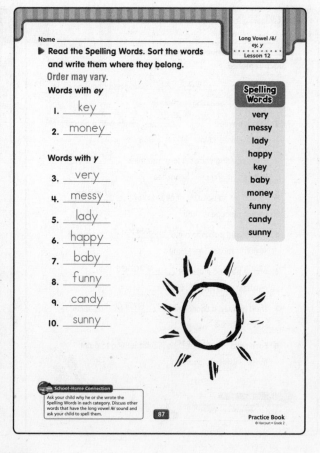

School-Home Connection
Ask your child why he or she wrote the Spelling Words in each category. Discuss other words that have the long vowel /ē/ sound and ask your child to spell them.

87

© Harcourt • Grade 2

Page 88

Name _____

▶ Read the passage. Then answer the questions and complete the chart.

Silly Games

Some games are silly. One silly game is called a sack race. For this game children put their legs into a big bag. Then they try to move by hopping. They race against other children wearing bags.

Another silly race is an egg and spoon race. For this race children carry a boiled egg on a spoon. They try to run to the finish line without dropping the egg.

Type of Writing	Author's Purpose	Clues
1. a report	2. It gives information about silly games.	3. The title is "Silly Games". 4. The author tells about two races.

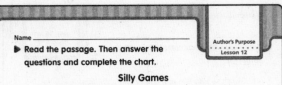
School-Home Connection
Read the passage with your child. Ask your child what would be different if, instead of giving information, the author's purpose were to tell a funny story about a sack race.

88

Practice Book
© Harcourt • Grade 2

Page 89

Name _____

▶ Finish the report. On each line, write a word from the box.

lazy	windy	dizzy	candy
copy	speedy	donkey	party

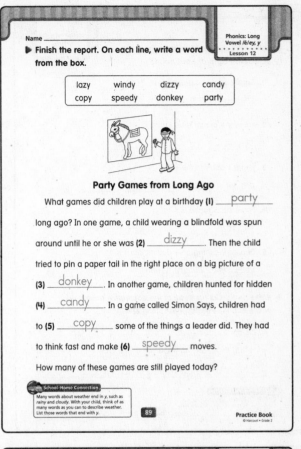

Party Games from Long Ago

What games did children play at a birthday (1) __party__ long ago? In one game, a child wearing a blindfold was spun around until he or she was (2) __dizzy__. Then the child tried to pin a paper tail in the right place on a big picture of a (3) __donkey__. In another game, children hunted for hidden (4) __candy__. In a game called Simon Says, children had to (5) __copy__ some of the things a leader did. They had to think fast and make (6) __speedy__ moves.

How many of these games are still played today?

School-Home Connection
Many words about weather end in y, such as rainy and cloudy. With your child, think of as many words as you can to describe weather. List those words that end with y.

89

Practice Book
© Harcourt • Grade 2

Page 90

Name _____

▶ Write the word from the box that completes the sentence.

imagine	favorite	year	enjoy
cook	board	popular	expensive

1. Chess is a game played on a __board__

2. Games of tag have been __popular__ with children for a long time.

3. Indoor games can be played all __year__

4. Some games are low cost, but others are __expensive__.

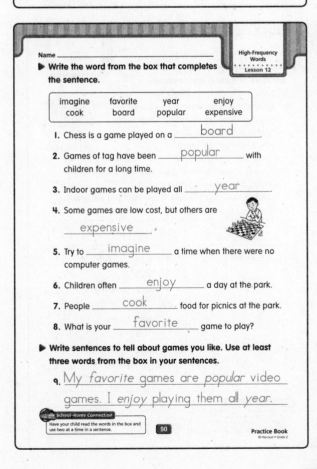

5. Try to __imagine__ a time when there were no computer games.

6. Children often __enjoy__ a day at the park.

7. People __cook__ food for picnics at the park.

8. What is your __favorite__ game to play?

▶ Write sentences to tell about games you like. Use at least three words from the box in your sentences.

9. My *favorite* games are *popular* video games. I *enjoy* playing them all *year.*

School-Home Connection
Have your child read the words in the box and use two at a time in a sentence.

90

Practice Book
© Harcourt • Grade 2

Page 91

Name _____

▶ Write the base word of the underlined word.

1. You can trade ten pennies for a dime. __penny__

2. Carly picked a bunch of daisies. __daisy__

3. Teddy tried to run a mile each day. __try__

4. We carried backpacks to school. __carry__

5. Dad fries eggs in a pan. __fry__

6. Sandy has been to three parties this week. __party__

7. We ate candied apples at the fair. __candy__

8. Snack on these sweet berries. __berry__

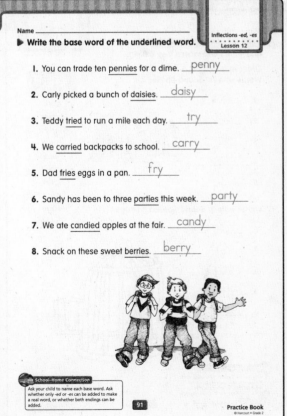

School-Home Connection
Ask your child to name each base word. Ask whether only -ed or -es can be added to make a real word, or whether both endings can be added.

91

Practice Book
© Harcourt • Grade 2

© Harcourt • Grade 2

Student Edition pp. 88–91

▶ Follow the directions to write the possessive form of each noun.

1. American + apostrophe + s

American's

2. country + apostrophe + s

country's

3. eagle + apostrophe + s

eagle's

4. flag + apostrophe + s

flag's

5. George Washington + apostrophe + s

George Washington's

▶ Write sentences for three of the possessive nouns you wrote above. **Possible responses are shown.**

6. Our country's name is the United States.

7. The eagle's wings are large.

8. The American flag's colors are red, white, and blue.

School-Home Connection
Point to three objects in your home. Ask your child to use a possessive noun to tell who owns each object.

92

Practice Book
© Harcourt • Grade 2

▶ Circle the word that completes each sentence.

1. Our class play is about a kind and _____ queen.

    judge   giggle   (gentle)

2. Gene plays the brave young _____.

    price   (prince)   print

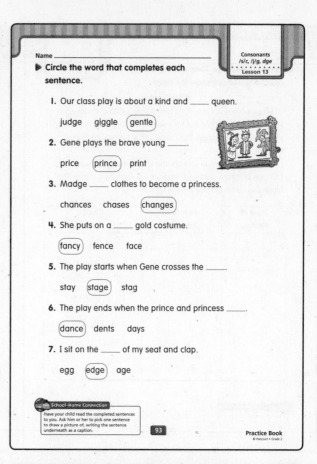

3. Madge _____ clothes to become a princess.

    chances   chases   (changes)

4. She puts on a _____ gold costume.

    (fancy)   fence   face

5. The play starts when Gene crosses the _____.

    stay   (stage)   stag

6. The play ends when the prince and princess _____.

    (dance)   dents   days

7. I sit on the _____ of my seat and clap.

    egg   (edge)   age

School-Home Connection
Have your child read the completed sentences to you. Ask him or her to pick one sentence to draw a picture of, writing the sentence underneath as a caption.

93

Practice Book
© Harcourt • Grade 2

▶ Read the Spelling Words. Sort the words and write them where they belong.

Order may vary.

Words with /s/ Sound Spelled c

1. slice

2. city

3. nice

4. space

5. price

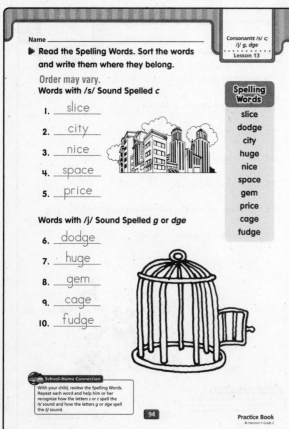

Spelling Words

slice
dodge
city
huge
nice
space
gem
price
cage
fudge

Words with /j/ Sound Spelled g or dge

6. dodge

7. huge

8. gem

9. cage

10. fudge

School-Home Connection
With your child, review the Spelling Words. Repeat each word and help him or her recognize how the letters s or c spell the /s/ sound and how the letters g or dge spell the /j/ sound.

94

Practice Book
© Harcourt • Grade 2

▶ Read the passage. Then answer the questions and complete the chart.

Mia's Wish

"I wish I were a teenager like my sister!" said Mia.

"Be careful what you wish for!" said a small voice behind her. Mia jumped.

"Who's talking?" she asked.

"I am!" said the voice. It came from close to her ear. Mia turned around. To her surprise, she saw a tiny man with silver wings. He was flying near her head!

"Don't be surprised," he said. "I can grant you any wish just by snapping my fingers!"

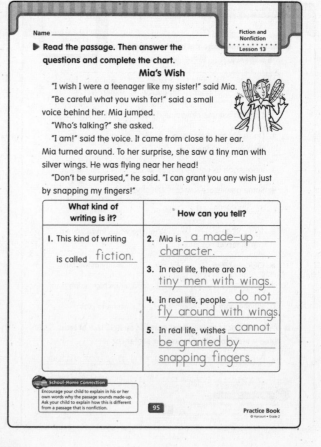

What kind of writing is it?	How can you tell?
1. This kind of writing is called fiction.	2. Mia is a made-up character.
	3. In real life, there are no tiny men with wings.
	4. In real life, people do not fly around with wings.
	5. In real life, wishes cannot be granted by snapping fingers.

School-Home Connection
Encourage your child to explain in his or her own words why the passage sounds made-up. Ask your child to explain how this is different from a passage that is nonfiction.

95

Practice Book
© Harcourt • Grade 2

Student Edition pp. 92–95

Top-left worksheet:

▶ Write each word from the box under the word with the same *c* or *g* sound.

cents	gift	gold	badge
acting	large	cotton	fancy
baggy	cap	lace	gems

fact	face	rag	rage
1. cotton	4. cents	7. gift	10. badge
2. cap	5. fancy	8. gold	11. large
3. acting	6. lace	9. baggy	12. gems

▶ Write some sentences about a costume you might wear in a play. Use at least one word from each list.

Possible response: My costume has a *fancy cap* with a feather. I also wear a *lace* shirt and *baggy, gold* pants covered with *gems*.

School-Home Connection
Have your child read each list and tell you why all the listed words belong there. Ask your child to read aloud the sentences about his or her costume, and then draw it.

96

Practice Book
© Harcourt • Grade 2

Top-right worksheet:

▶ Write the word from the box that completes the sentence.

wash	woman	above	shoes
tough	young	wear	

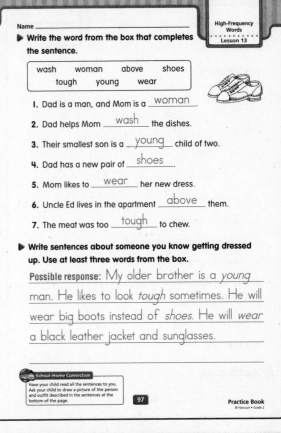

1. Dad is a man, and Mom is a _woman_.
2. Dad helps Mom _wash_ the dishes.
3. Their smallest son is a _young_ child of two.
4. Dad has a new pair of _shoes_.
5. Mom likes to _wear_ her new dress.
6. Uncle Ed lives in the apartment _above_ them.
7. The meat was too _tough_ to chew.

▶ Write sentences about someone you know getting dressed up. Use at least three words from the box.

Possible response: My older brother is a *young* man. He likes to look *tough* sometimes. He will wear big boots instead of *shoes*. He will *wear* a black leather jacket and sunglasses.

School-Home Connection
Have your child read all the sentences to you. Ask your child to draw a picture of the person and outfit described in the sentences at the bottom of the page.

97

Practice Book
© Harcourt • Grade 2

Bottom-left worksheet:

▶ Add the ending *-ed* or *-ing* to the base word to complete the sentence. Write the word on the line.

1. Our class was _planning_ to put on a play.
   plan
2. We kept _changing_ our parts.
   change
3. Lin _bragged_ that she knew all the lines.
   brag
4. Ramon kept _fussing_ with the props.
   fuss
5. Meg and Lucas never _stopped_ talking.
   stop
6. Tonya and Rosa were _dancing_ around.
   dance
7. Our teacher _clapped_ her hands.
   clap
8. "Let's settle down!" she _called_ out.
   call
9. She _nodded_ when we got back to work.
   nod

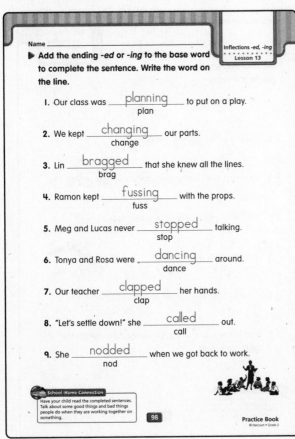

School-Home Connection
Have your child read the completed sentences. Talk about some good things and bad things people do when they are working together on something.

98

Practice Book
© Harcourt • Grade 2

Bottom-right worksheet:

▶ Complete each sentence with a plural possessive noun from the box.

Tigers'	girls'	workers'
teachers'	animals'	ladies'

1. The _workers'_ locker room is big.
2. The _ladies'_ group is for women only.
3. The supply room is only for _teachers'_ supplies.
4. The _Tigers'_ locker room was painted orange and black.
5. The _girls'_ bags said *Dynamite Dancers*.
6. The _animals'_ cages were cleaned this morning.

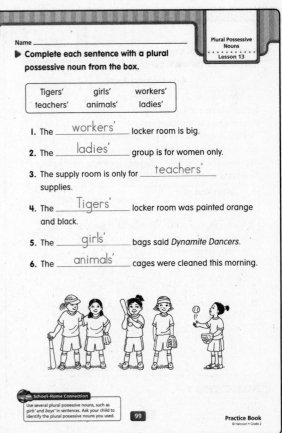

School-Home Connection
Use several plural possessive nouns, such as *girls'* and *boys'* in sentences. Ask your child to identify the plural possessive nouns you used.

99

Practice Book
© Harcourt • Grade 2

Name _____

▶ Write the letter of the sentence that goes with the picture.

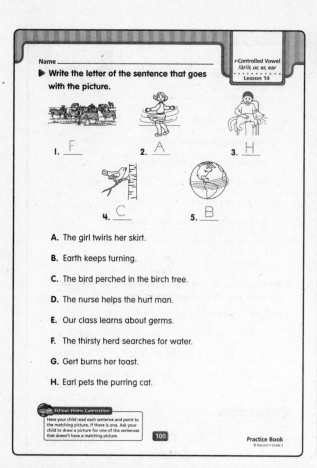

1. _F_ 2. _A_ 3. _H_

4. _C_ 5. _B_

A. The girl twirls her skirt.

B. Earth keeps turning.

C. The bird perched in the birch tree.

D. The nurse helps the hurt man.

E. Our class learns about germs.

F. The thirsty herd searches for water.

G. Gert burns her toast.

H. Earl pets the purring cat.

Name _____

▶ Read the Spelling Words. Sort the words and write them where they belong.
Order may vary.

Words with /ûr/ Sound Spelled *ir*

1. shirt
2. stir
3. bird
4. third

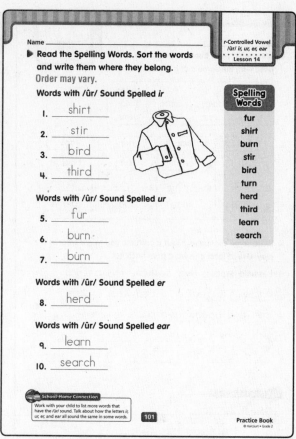

Words with /ûr/ Sound Spelled *ur*

5. fur
6. burn
7. burn

Words with /ûr/ Sound Spelled *er*

8. herd

Words with /ûr/ Sound Spelled *ear*

9. learn
10. search

Spelling Words
fur
shirt
burn
stir
bird
turn
herd
third
learn
search

Name _____

▶ Read the passage. Then answer the questions and complete the chart.

Gila Monster Facts

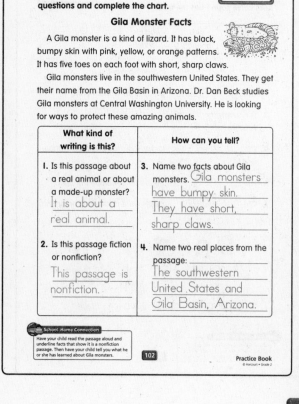

A Gila monster is a kind of lizard. It has black, bumpy skin with pink, yellow, or orange patterns. It has five toes on each foot with short, sharp claws.

Gila monsters live in the southwestern United States. They get their name from the Gila Basin in Arizona. Dr. Dan Beck studies Gila monsters at Central Washington University. He is looking for ways to protect these amazing animals.

What kind of writing is this?	How can you tell?
1. Is this passage about a real animal or about a made-up monster? It is about a real animal.	3. Name two facts about Gila monsters. Gila monsters have bumpy skin. They have short, sharp claws.
2. Is this passage fiction or nonfiction? This passage is nonfiction.	4. Name two real places from the passage: The southwestern United States and Gila Basin, Arizona.

Name _____

▶ Circle and write the one word in each sentence that has the same vowel + r sound you hear in *learn*.

1. Most of the animals on the (earth) are found in rain forests.
   earth

2. Many (birds) live in a rain forest.
   birds

3. Marmoset dads teach their babies how to (search) for food.
   search

4. Elephants have big ears and live in (herds).
   herds

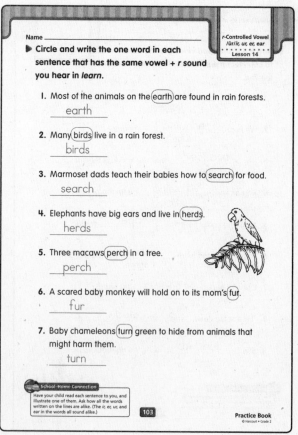

5. Three macaws (perch) in a tree.
   perch

6. A scared baby monkey will hold on to its mom's (fur).
   fur

7. Baby chameleons (turn) green to hide from animals that might harm them.
   turn

Student Edition pp. 100–103

▶ **Complete the paragraph with words from the box.**

sweat	thumb	father
touch	care	interesting

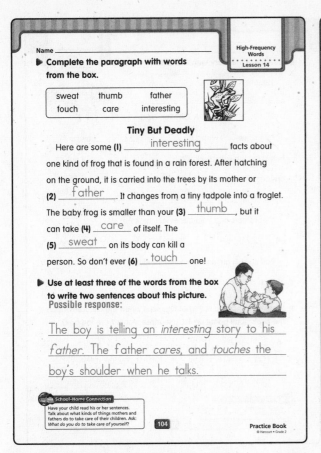

Tiny But Deadly

Here are some **(1)** ___interesting___ facts about one kind of frog that is found in a rain forest. After hatching on the ground, it is carried into the trees by its mother or **(2)** ___father___. It changes from a tiny tadpole into a froglet. The baby frog is smaller than your **(3)** ___thumb___, but it can take **(4)** ___care___ of itself. The **(5)** ___sweat___ on its body can kill a person. So don't ever **(6)** ___touch___ one!

▶ **Use at least three of the words from the box to write two sentences about this picture.**
Possible response:

___The boy is telling an interesting story to his father. The father cares, and touches the boy's shoulder when he talks.___

104

Practice Book
© Harcourt • Grade 2

▶ **Below each sentence are three syllables. Put two together to make a word that fits. Write it on the line.**

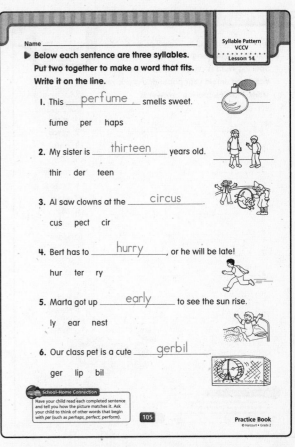

1. This ___perfume___ smells sweet.

   fume   per   haps

2. My sister is ___thirteen___ years old.

   thir   der   teen

3. Al saw clowns at the ___circus___.

   cus   pect   cir

4. Bert has to ___hurry___, or he will be late!

   hur   ter   ry

5. Marta got up ___early___ to see the sun rise.

   ly   ear   nest

6. Our class pet is a cute ___gerbil___.

   ger   lip   bil

105

Practice Book
© Harcourt • Grade 2

▶ **Read each sentence. Circle the pronoun that completes each sentence.**

1. Do (you, I) want to go to the movies with us?

2. (It, We) are going out to eat, too.

3. (She, Me) is going to ride with Carmen and Maya.

4. (They, He) are going in the van with Sarah.

5. (It, You) is a funny movie.

▶ **Read each sentence. Replace the underlined noun with a pronoun. Then write the new sentence.**

6. Pigs like to roll in the mud.

   ___They like to roll in the mud.___

7. The mud cools them off on hot days.

   ___It cools them off on hot days.___

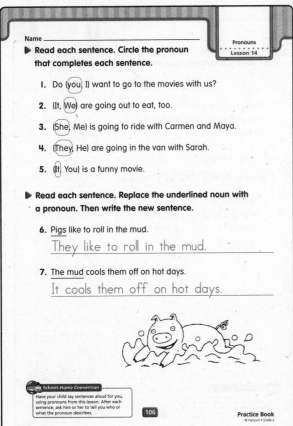

106

Practice Book
© Harcourt • Grade 2

▶ **Circle and write the word that completes each sentence.**

1. Mom wants to ___teach___ me to paint walls.

   teeth   trash   (teach)

2. I have a fat brush, and Mom has a ___thin___ brush.

   chin   (thin)   shin

3. The color of this paint ___matches___ my red socks.

   (matches)   mashes   math

4. After I paint, I will take a ___bath___ to get clean.

   batch   (bath)   bush

▶ **Below each sentence are three syllables. Put two of them together to make the correct word. Write it on the line.**

5. A ___chipmunk___ has a stripe on its back.

   munk   chip   fish

6. Sela kept ___rubbing___ her sore ear.

   rub   bing   bish

7. Lee and Lin cleaned up all by ___themselves___.

   him   them   selves

8. Can you help Mitch solve his ___problem___?

   mis   lem   prob

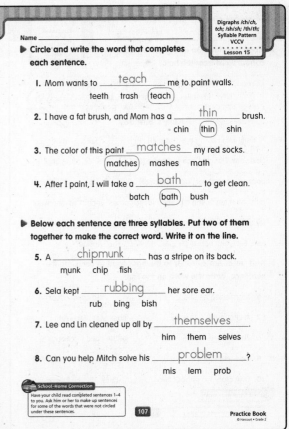

107

Practice Book
© Harcourt • Grade 2

29

Student Edition pp. 104–107

Name _____

▶ Fold the page along the dotted line. As each Spelling Word is called out, write it on the line. Then unfold your paper and check your work. Practice spelling any words you missed.

Spelling Words

1. wish
2. catch
3. bath
4. very
5. money
6. huge
7. price
8. stir
9. turn
10. learn

1. _____
2. _____
3. _____
4. _____
5. _____
6. _____
7. _____
8. _____
9. _____
10. _____

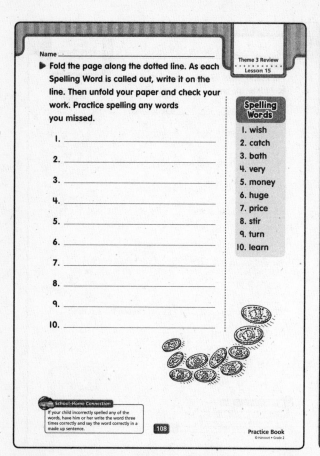

School-Home Connection
If your child incorrectly spelled any of the words, have him or her write the word three times correctly and say the word correctly in a made up sentence.

108

Practice Book
© Harcourt • Grade 2

Name _____

▶ Complete the story with words from the box.

| bought | expensive | favorite |
| young | father | |

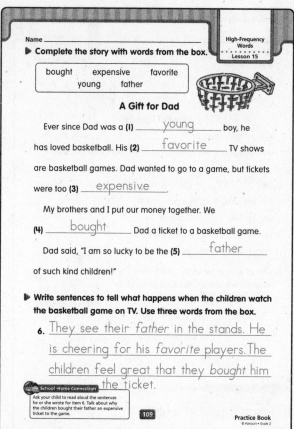

A Gift for Dad

Ever since Dad was a (1) ___young___ boy, he has loved basketball. His (2) ___favorite___ TV shows are basketball games. Dad wanted to go to a game, but tickets were too (3) ___expensive___.

My brothers and I put our money together. We (4) ___bought___ Dad a ticket to a basketball game.

Dad said, "I am so lucky to be the (5) ___father___ of such kind children!"

▶ Write sentences to tell what happens when the children watch the basketball game on TV. Use three words from the box.

6. They see their *father* in the stands. He is cheering for his *favorite* players. The children feel great that they *bought* him the ticket.

School-Home Connection
Ask your child to read aloud the sentences he or she wrote for item 6. Talk about why the children bought their father an expensive ticket to the game.

109

Practice Book
© Harcourt • Grade 2

Name _____

▶ Finish the story. On each line, write the correct word from the box.

| many | hurry | bushy | handy | party |
| key | valley | donkey | berry | |

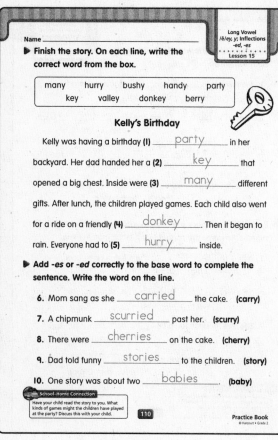

Kelly's Birthday

Kelly was having a birthday (1) ___party___ in her backyard. Her dad handed her a (2) ___key___ that opened a big chest. Inside were (3) ___many___ different gifts. After lunch, the children played games. Each child also went for a ride on a friendly (4) ___donkey___. Then it began to rain. Everyone had to (5) ___hurry___ inside.

▶ Add -es or -ed correctly to the base word to complete the sentence. Write the word on the line.

6. Mom sang as she ___carried___ the cake. (carry)

7. A chipmunk ___scurried___ past her. (scurry)

8. There were ___cherries___ on the cake. (cherry)

9. Dad told funny ___stories___ to the children. (story)

10. One story was about two ___babies___ (baby)

School-Home Connection
Have your child read the story to you. What kinds of games might the children have played at the party? Discuss this with your child.

110

Practice Book
© Harcourt • Grade 2

Name _____

▶ Read the passage. Then fill in the chart to tell about the author's purpose.

Art Class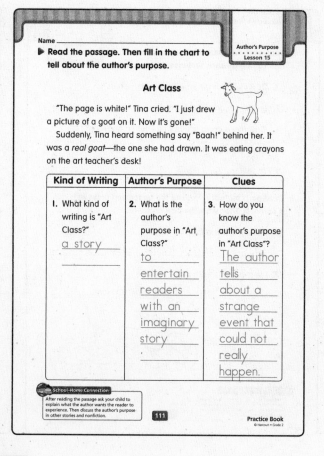

"The page is white!" Tina cried. "I just drew a picture of a goat on it. Now it's gone!"

Suddenly, Tina heard something say "Baah!" behind her. It was a *real goat*—the one she had drawn. It was eating crayons on the art teacher's desk!

Kind of Writing	Author's Purpose	Clues
1. What kind of writing is "Art Class?" a story	2. What is the author's purpose in "Art Class?" to entertain readers with an imaginary story	3. How do you know the author's purpose in "Art Class"? The author tells about a strange event that could not really happen.

School-Home Connection
After reading the passage ask your child to explain what the author wants the reader to experience. Then discuss the author's purpose in other stories and nonfiction.

111

Practice Book
© Harcourt • Grade 2

▶ Write the word from the box that completes the sentence.

| minute | care | above |
| interesting | imagine | |

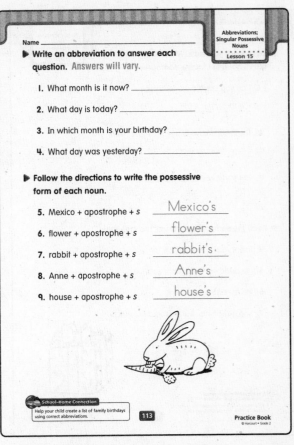

1. In just a _____minute_____, a baby bird will hatch.

2. It is hard to _____imagine_____ that such a tiny, weak bird will grow to be big and strong.

3. The mother bird flies _____above_____ the nest.

4. Birds take good _____care_____ of their babies.

5. It is _____interesting_____ to learn about baby birds.

▶ Write sentences to describe baby birds or baby animals. Use at least two of the words from the box.

6. It is *interesting* to *imagine* a baby bird learning to fly. It takes off from high *above* the ground and doesn't seem afraid.

School-Home Connection
Ask your child to read aloud his or her sentences for item 6. Together, come up with a good question related to the topic, and talk about how to find an answer.

112

Practice Book
© Harcourt • Grade 2

▶ Write an abbreviation to answer each question. **Answers will vary.**

1. What month is it now? _____

2. What day is today? _____

3. In which month is your birthday? _____

4. What day was yesterday? _____

▶ Follow the directions to write the possessive form of each noun.

5. Mexico + apostrophe + s _____Mexico's_____

6. flower + apostrophe + s _____flower's_____

7. rabbit + apostrophe + s _____rabbit's_____

8. Anne + apostrophe + s _____Anne's_____

9. house + apostrophe + s _____house's_____

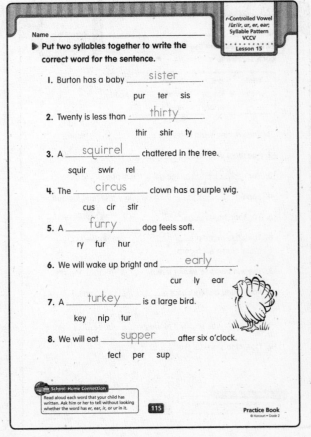

School-Home Connection
Help your child create a list of family birthdays using correct abbreviations.

113

Practice Book
© Harcourt • Grade 2

▶ Move each word from the box to the chart. Match each word to the same c or g sound.

| edge | race | coat | cent |
| gave | gentle | carve | ugly |

fact	face	rag	rage
1. carve	2. cent	3. gave	4. edge
5. coat	6. race	7. ugly	8. gentle

▶ Add -ed or -ing correctly to the base word to complete the sentence. Write the word on the line.

9. Glen was _____sitting_____ next to Mom. **(sit)**

10. Mom was _____cutting_____ his hair. **(cut)**

11. She _____trimmed_____ the back. **(trim)**

12. Then Mom _____hugged_____ Glen. **(hug)**

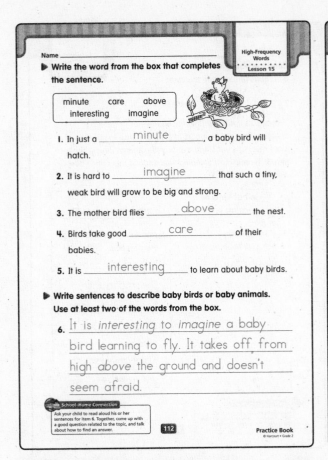

School-Home Connection
Give your child these words to add to the chart at the top of the page: cave, ice, gold, huge, green, range, city, cup. Each list will be two words longer.

114

Practice Book
© Harcourt • Grade 2

▶ Put two syllables together to write the correct word for the sentence.

1. Burton has a baby _____sister_____
   pur ter sis

2. Twenty is less than _____thirty_____
   thir shir ty

3. A _____squirrel_____ chattered in the tree.
   squir swir rel

4. The _____circus_____ clown has a purple wig.
   cus cir stir

5. A _____furry_____ dog feels soft.
   ry fur hur

6. We will wake up bright and _____early_____.
   cur ly ear

7. A _____turkey_____ is a large bird.
   key nip tur

8. We will eat _____supper_____ after six o'clock.
   fect per sup

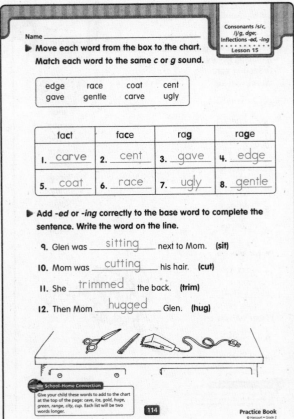

School-Home Connection
Read aloud each word that your child has written. Ask him or her to tell without looking whether the word has er, ear, ir, or ur in it.

115

Practice Book
© Harcourt • Grade 2

Plural Possessive Nouns; Pronouns
Lesson 15

▶ Write each sentence. Make the plural noun in ( ) show ownership.

1. Can you see the (lions) den?

   Can you see the lions' den?

2. The (bears) cave is beyond those trees.

   The bears' cave is beyond those trees.

3. The (girls) costumes are ready.

   The girls' costumes are ready.

▶ Read the sentences. Circle all the pronouns.

4. (I) sent Alex a present.

5. (He) could not tell what (it) was.

6. (He) asked Sally about (it).

7. (She) gave hints, but (he) could not guess.

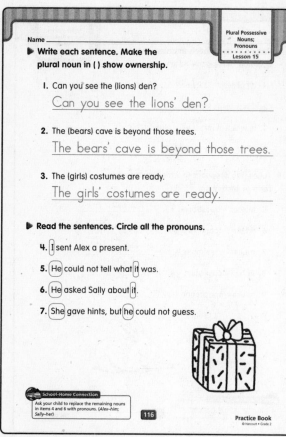

Name _____

Fiction and Nonfiction
Lesson 15

▶ Read the passage. Then answer the questions to complete the chart.

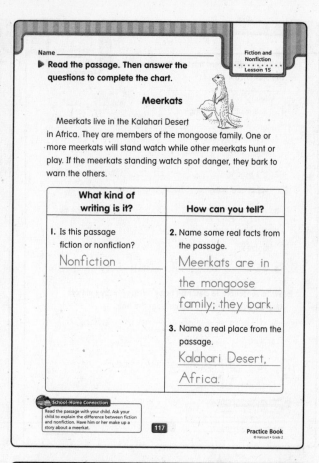

Meerkats

Meerkats live in the Kalahari Desert in Africa. They are members of the mongoose family. One or more meerkats will stand watch while other meerkats hunt or play. If the meerkats standing watch spot danger, they bark to warn the others.

What kind of writing is it?	How can you tell?
1. Is this passage fiction or nonfiction? Nonfiction	2. Name some real facts from the passage. Meerkats are in the mongoose family; they bark. 3. Name a real place from the passage. Kalahari Desert, Africa.

Name _____

Digraphs /n/kn; /r/wr; /f/gh, ph
Lesson 16

▶ Write a word from the box to complete each sentence.

knot	graph	tough	wrecked
wrote	laugh	photo	wrapped
	trophy	knight	

1. The winning team takes the ___trophy___ home.

2. The meat was too ___tough___ to chew.

3. We ___wrapped___ the gift in fancy paper.

4. Sophie ___wrote___ a funny story and read it aloud.

5. The rope has a ___knot___ in it.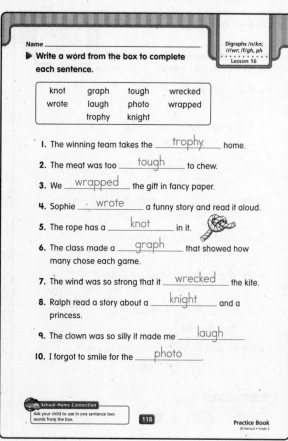

6. The class made a ___graph___ that showed how many chose each game.

7. The wind was so strong that it ___wrecked___ the kite.

8. Ralph read a story about a ___knight___ and a princess.

9. The clown was so silly it made me ___laugh___.

10. I forgot to smile for the ___photo___.

Name _____

Consonant Digraphs /n/ kn, /r/ wr, /f/ gh, ph
Lesson 16

▶ Read the Spelling Words. Sort the words and write them where they belong.
Order may vary.

Words with kn

1. knot
2. know
3. knife

Words with wr

4. wrong
5. wreck
6. wrap

Words with gh

7. tough
8. laugh

Words with ph

9. graph
10. phone

Spelling Words

knot
wrong
know
wreck
graph
wrap
knife
tough
phone
laugh

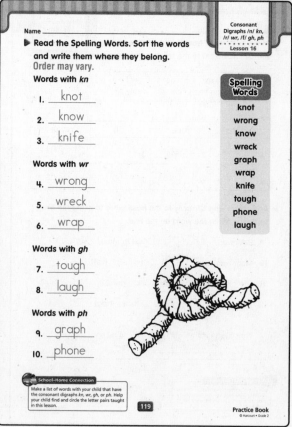

▶ Read the story. Then answer the questions to complete the chart.

Tam's Idea

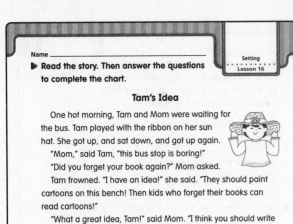

One hot morning, Tam and Mom were waiting for the bus. Tam played with the ribbon on her sun hat. She got up, and sat down, and got up again.

"Mom," said Tam, "this bus stop is boring!"

"Did you forget your book again?" Mom asked.

Tam frowned. "I have an idea!" she said. "They should paint cartoons on this bench! Then kids who forget their books can read cartoons!"

"What a great idea, Tam!" said Mom. "I think you should write and tell our city mayor about your idea!"

Setting	Clues
1. Where does this story happen? a bus stop in the city	3. Which words tell you where the story happens? bus stop, city mayor
2. When does this story happen? in the summer	4. Which words tell you when the story happens? one hot morning

School-Home Connection
Have your child read the story to you. Ask him or her to explain how the words give clues about when and where the story happens.

120

Practice Book
© Harcourt • Grade 2

Name _____

Digraphs /n/kn;
/r/wr; /f/gh, ph
Lesson 16

▶ Circle the word that completes each sentence. Write it on the line.

1. I know which answer is ___ wrong ___
   knot   write   (wrong)

2. Knock on the door, and turn the ___ knob ___
   rough   (knob)   phone

3. Phil ___ laughs ___ at the silly photo.
   (laughs)   knocks   wraps

4. Children learn the alphabet and ___ phonics ___
   (phonics)   elephant   wrinkle

5. The yarn in the ___ knitting ___ basket is knotted.
   phoning   (knitting)   kneeling

6. Have you written ___ enough ___ in your story, or should you tell more?
   rough   graph   (enough)

7. The nurse wrapped a bandage around my hurt ___ wrist ___.
   (wrist)   knelt   cough

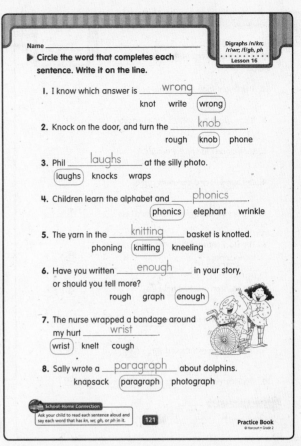

8. Sally wrote a ___ paragraph ___ about dolphins.
   knapsack   (paragraph)   photograph

School-Home Connection
Ask your child to read each sentence aloud and say each word that has kn, wr, gh, or ph in it.

121

Practice Book
© Harcourt • Grade 2

▶ Write the word that answers the question.

1. Which word goes with instead?
   ___ another ___
   another   easy   outside

2. Which word goes with enchanting?
   ___ charming ___
   expensive   frightening   charming

3. Which word goes with thrilled?
   ___ delight ___
   delight   hidden   throwing

4. Which word goes with cozy?
   ___ blanket ___
   computer   plate   blanket

5. Which word goes with review?
   ___ judging ___
   spinning   judging   whispering

6. Which word goes with celebrate?
   ___ party ___
   party   monkey   winter

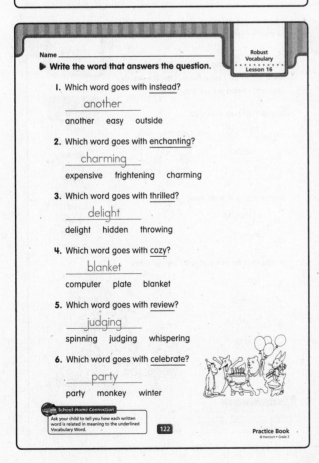

School-Home Connection
Ask your child to tell you how each written word is related in meaning to the underlined Vocabulary Word.

122

Practice Book
© Harcourt • Grade 2

▶ Read the directions. Look at the map. Then answer the questions.

Wild Animal Park Map

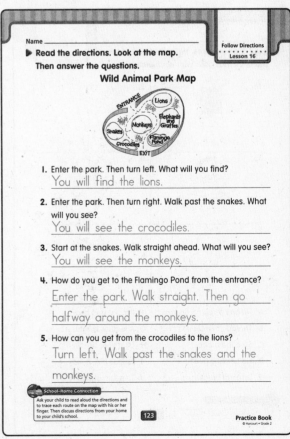

1. Enter the park. Then turn left. What will you find?
   You will find the lions.

2. Enter the park. Then turn right. Walk past the snakes. What will you see?
   You will see the crocodiles.

3. Start at the snakes. Walk straight ahead. What will you see?
   You will see the monkeys.

4. How do you get to the Flamingo Pond from the entrance?
   Enter the park. Walk straight. Then go halfway around the monkeys.

5. How can you get from the crocodiles to the lions?
   Turn left. Walk past the snakes and the monkeys.

School-Home Connection
Ask your child to read aloud the directions and to trace each route on the map with his or her finger. Then discuss directions from your home to your child's school.

123

Practice Book
© Harcourt • Grade 2

Suffixes -ly, -ness
Lesson 16

▶ Write the base word of the underlined word.

1. The knight rode <u>bravely</u> into battle. brave

2. If you speak too <u>softly</u>, I can't hear you. soft

3. Look <u>closely</u> to see the details. close

4. The sun set, and <u>darkness</u> came. dark

5. Thank you for your <u>kindness</u> and help. kind

6. The story showed that hard work is better than <u>laziness</u>. lazy

7. The children laughed <u>happily</u>. happy

8. Steel is known for its <u>toughness</u>. tough

9. The line for lunch moved very <u>slowly</u>. slow

10. The kitten loved the <u>softness</u> of the blanket. soft

School-Home Connection
Ask your child to tell what each sentence means, using the base word in the explanation.

124

Practice Book
© Harcourt • Grade 2

Adjectives
Lesson 16

▶ Read the sentences. Circle the adjective in each sentence. If the adjective tells about color, write *color*. If it tells about shape, write *shape*. If it tells about size, write *size*.

1. I like to build with (big) blocks. size

2. Sara likes to build with (small) cubes. size

3. The blocks are (yellow). color

4. I need a (square) block. shape

▶ Read the paragraph. Choose a word from the box to complete each sentence. Write it on the line.

| little | long | tall |

I like to play in the sand at the beach. First I make a
(5) ___tall___ castle. Then I make (6) ___long___
roads around it. My sister likes to make lots of (7) ___little___
houses. After playing in the sand, we get to jump in the cool
ocean water.

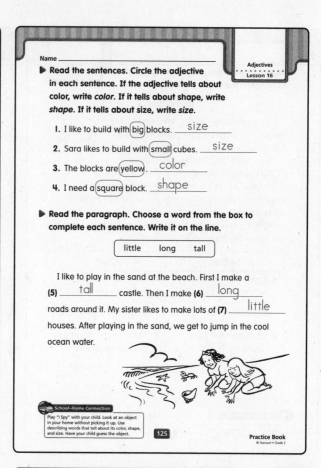

School-Home Connection
Play "I Spy" with your child. Look at an object in your home without picking it up. Use describing words that tell about its color, shape, and size. Have your child guess the object.

125

Practice Book
© Harcourt • Grade 2

Short Vowel /e/ea
Lesson 17

▶ Read the sentences. Write the letter of the sentence that goes with each picture.

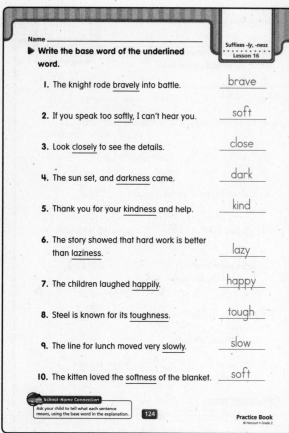

1. B
2. F
3. H
4. E
5. C
6. A

A He has a cap on his head.
B Thread the needle.
C Slice the bread.
D He has fine health.
E Let's eat breakfast.

F It is big and heavy.
G A feather is light.
H Hold your breath.
I Its legs are steady.
J They run ahead.

School-Home Connection
Have your child read each sentence aloud and point out or describe a picture for each one.

126

Practice Book
© Harcourt • Grade 2

Short Vowel /e/ ea
Lesson 17

▶ Make cards for the Spelling Words. Lay them down and read them. Sort the words and write them where they belong.

Spelling Words

heavy
steady
bread
sweat
head
thread
breath
ready
meant
health

Words that end with *ead*

1. bread
2. head
3. thread

Words that end with *eady*

4. steady
5. ready

Words that do not end with *ead* or *eady*

6. heavy
7. sweat
8. breath
9. meant
10. health

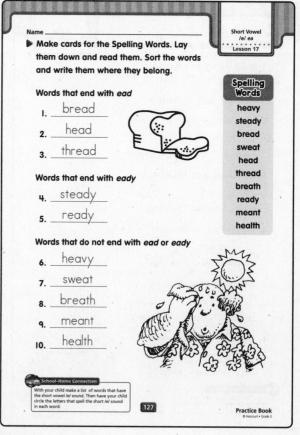

School-Home Connection
With your child make a list of words that have the short vowel /e/ sound. Then have your child circle the letters that spell the short /e/ sound in each word.

127

Practice Book
© Harcourt • Grade 2

Student Edition pp. 124–127

© Harcourt • Grade 2

Page 128

▶ **Read each passage. Then answer the questions.**

"I wish I had super-swimmer arms like you, Alicia," said Marty, trying to keep up.

Just then Marty noticed something.

"Look! A dolphin!" he shouted.

"You don't have super-swimmer arms yet, but you do have super-swimmer eyes!" said Alicia.

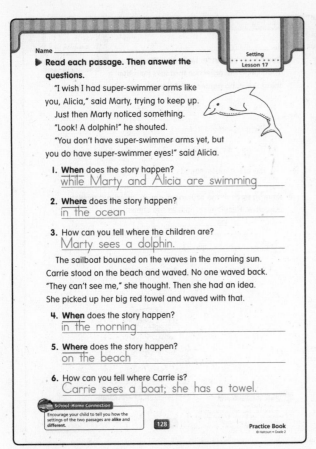

1. When does the story happen?
while Marty and Alicia are swimming

2. Where does the story happen?
in the ocean

3. How can you tell where the children are?
Marty sees a dolphin.

The sailboat bounced on the waves in the morning sun. Carrie stood on the beach and waved. No one waved back. "They can't see me," she thought. Then she had an idea. She picked up her big red towel and waved with that.

4. When does the story happen?
in the morning

5. Where does the story happen?
on the beach

6. How can you tell where Carrie is?
Carrie sees a boat; she has a towel.

School-Home Connection
Encourage your child to tell you how the settings of the two passages are **alike** and **different.**

128

Practice Book
© Harcourt • Grade 2

Page 129

▶ **Circle the word in each sentence that has the same vowel sound as *head*. Write it on the line**

1. Jean is (ready) to be seated.
ready

2. We need heat in cold (weather).
weather

3. (Breakfast) is the first meal of the day.
Breakfast

4. Dogs run and leap to stay fit and (healthy).
healthy

5. Dean keeps his feet (steady) on a ladder.
steady

6. This (bread) is made from wheat.
bread

7. Gene (spread) peanut butter on his toast.
spread

8. The bird has a sharp beak and black (feathers).
feathers

9. Will you please (thread) this needle for Pete?
thread

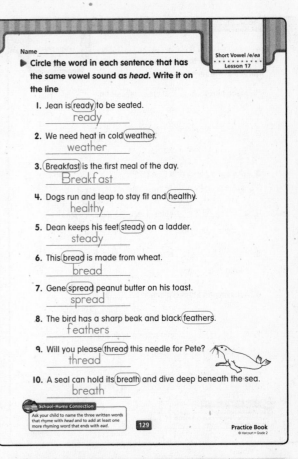

10. A seal can hold its (breath) and dive deep beneath the sea.
breath

School-Home Connection
Ask your child to name the three written words that rhyme with *head* and to add at least one more rhyming word that ends with *ead*.

129

Practice Book
© Harcourt • Grade 2

Page 130

▶ **Write two words from the box that go with each Vocabulary Word.**

play	drank	besides	easy
kicked	yelling	squeaking	sing
marched	without	happy	tasted

1. stomped
kicked
marched

2. sipped
drank
tasted

3. entertain
play
sing

4. except
without
besides

5. carefree
easy
happy

6. screeching
yelling
squeaking

▶ **Choose two Vocabulary Words. Write each of them in a sentence. Responses will vary.**

7. _____

_____

8. _____

_____

School-Home Connection
Ask your child to show the meaning of each numbered word, without using any words. You try to guess which word is being performed.

130

Practice Book
© Harcourt • Grade 2

Page 131

How to Make Lemonade

▶ **Read the directions. Then answer the questions.**

What You Need
- a large pitcher
- 1 cup of sugar
- ice
- 5 cups of water
- 6 lemons

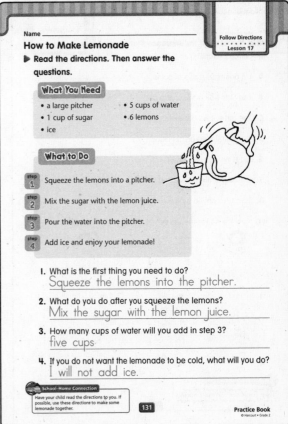

What to Do

step 1 Squeeze the lemons into a pitcher.

step 2 Mix the sugar with the lemon juice.

step 3 Pour the water into the pitcher.

step 4 Add ice and enjoy your lemonade!

1. What is the first thing you need to do?
Squeeze the lemons into the pitcher.

2. What do you do after you squeeze the lemons?
Mix the sugar with the lemon juice.

3. How many cups of water will you add in step 3?
five cups

4. If you do not want the lemonade to be cold, what will you do?
I will not add ice.

School-Home Connection
Have your child read the directions to you. If possible, use these directions to make some lemonade together.

131

Practice Book
© Harcourt • Grade 2

© Harcourt • Grade 2

Panel 1 (page 132)

▶ Put two syllables together to write a word that fits in the sentence.

1. Jason plays ____music____ in a band.
   sic tu mu

2. Every ____student____ in the class is here.
   stu dent sut

3. Take out a pencil and ____paper____.
   pa fi per

4. A ____spider____ spins a web.
   der spi ta

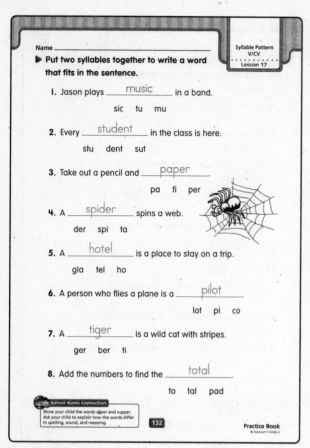

5. A ____hotel____ is a place to stay on a trip.
   gla tel ho

6. A person who flies a plane is a ____pilot____.
   lot pi co

7. A ____tiger____ is a wild cat with stripes.
   ger ber ti

8. Add the numbers to find the ____total____.
   to tal pad

School-Home Connection
Show your child the words *sipper* and *supper*. Ask your child to explain how the words differ in spelling, sound, and meaning.

132

Practice Book
© Harcourt • Grade 2

Panel 2 (page 133)

▶ Read each sentence. Underline the noun. Then circle the adjective that tells how the thing the noun names smells, tastes, sounds, or feels.

1. The coffee tastes bitter.

2. The grass smells fresh.

3. The raincoat feels slick.

4. The piano music sounds soft.

▶ Rewrite each of the sentences above, using a different adjective. Possible responses are shown.

5. The coffee tastes good.

6. The grass smells sweet.

7. The raincoat feels smooth.

8. The piano music sounds loud.

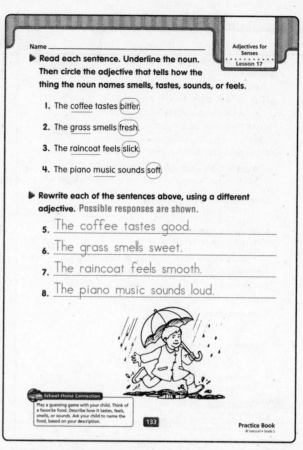

School-Home Connection
Play a guessing game with your child. Think of a favorite food. Describe how it tastes, feels, smells, or sounds. Ask your child to name the food, based on your description.

133

Practice Book
© Harcourt • Grade 2

Panel 3 (page 134)

▶ Write the letter of the sentence that goes with each picture.

A. He points to a pile of coins.

B. The little boy is filled with joy.

C. The girl enjoys her new toys.

D. Troy just joined an art club.

E. Joy is being very noisy!

F. The oil painting is spoiled.

G. Sam is annoyed by the rain.

H. Now the soil in the garden is moist.

1. C   2. G   3. H

4. E   5. A

School-Home Connection
Have your child read the sentence that goes with each picture. Ask your child to choose one of the sentences that was not used and draw a picture to go with it.

134

Practice Book
© Harcourt • Grade 2

Panel 4 (page 135)

▶ Read the Spelling Words. Sort them and write them where they belong.

Words with oi

1. join
2. boil
3. soil
4. noise
5. voice
6. point
7. coin

Words with oy

8. joy
9. boy
10. toy

Spelling Words

join
boil
joy
soil
noise
boy
voice
point
toy
coin

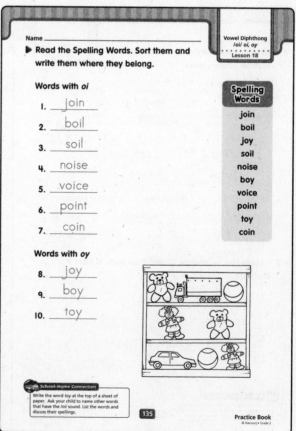

School-Home Connection
Write the word *toy* at the top of a sheet of paper. Ask your child to name other words that have the /oi/ sound. List the words and discuss their spellings.

135

Practice Book
© Harcourt • Grade 2

Student Edition pp. 132–135

© Harcourt • Grade 2

▶ **Read the table of contents. Then answer the questions.**

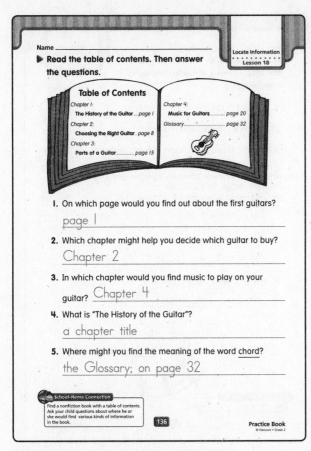

Table of Contents

1. On which page would you find out about the first guitars?

   page 1

2. Which chapter might help you decide which guitar to buy?

   Chapter 2

3. In which chapter would you find music to play on your guitar? Chapter 4

4. What is "The History of the Guitar"?

   a chapter title

5. Where might you find the meaning of the word chord?

   the Glossary; on page 32

136

▶ **Finish the story. On each line, write a word from the box. You will not use all the words.**

coins	noisy	boy	choice
enjoys	point	voice	toy

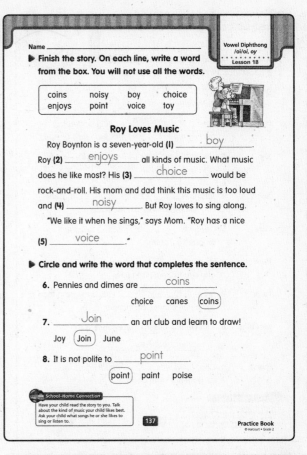

Roy Loves Music

Roy Boynton is a seven-year-old (1) ___boy___.

Roy (2) ___enjoys___ all kinds of music. What music does he like most? His (3) ___choice___ would be rock-and-roll. His mom and dad think this music is too loud and (4) ___noisy___. But Roy loves to sing along.

"We like it when he sings," says Mom. "Roy has a nice

(5) ___voice___."

▶ **Circle and write the word that completes the sentence.**

6. Pennies and dimes are ___coins___.

   choice   canes   (coins)

7. ___Join___ an art club and learn to draw!

   Joy   (Join)   June

8. It is not polite to ___point___

   (point)   paint   poise

137

▶ **Write the word that best answers the question.**

1. Which word goes with creative? ___artist___
   artist   farmer   nurse

2. Which word goes with relieved? ___glad___
   glad   sad   mad

3. Which word goes with expression? ___face___
   knees   hair   face

4. Which word goes with volume? ___sound___
   sight   smell   sound

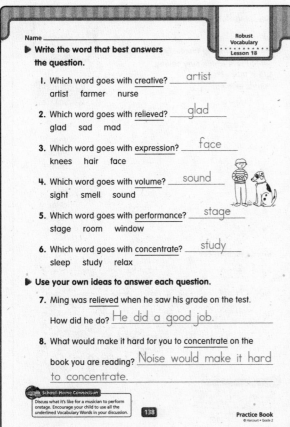

5. Which word goes with performance? ___stage___
   stage   room   window

6. Which word goes with concentrate? ___study___
   sleep   study   relax

▶ **Use your own ideas to answer each question.**

7. Ming was relieved when he saw his grade on the test.

   How did he do? He did a good job.

8. What would make it hard for you to concentrate on the

   book you are reading? Noise would make it hard to concentrate.

138

▶ **Choose the reference source or sources you would use to find the information.**

encyclopedia	atlas	map
dictionary	thesaurus	Internet

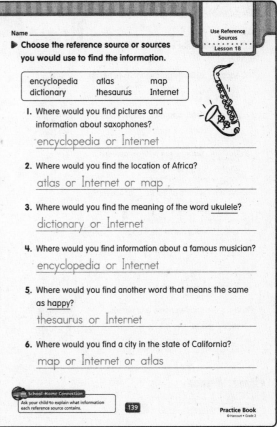

1. Where would you find pictures and information about saxophones?

   encyclopedia or Internet

2. Where would you find the location of Africa?

   atlas or Internet or map

3. Where would you find the meaning of the word ukulele?

   dictionary or Internet

4. Where would you find information about a famous musician?

   encyclopedia or Internet

5. Where would you find another word that means the same as happy?

   thesaurus or Internet

6. Where would you find a city in the state of California?

   map or Internet or atlas

139

Name _____

▶ Add *-ful* or *-less* to the base word to complete the sentence. Write the word on the line.

grace   1. The _____graceful_____ girl dances very well.

rest   2. The _____restless_____ boy kept moving around.

joy   3. The class sang a happy, _____joyful_____ song.

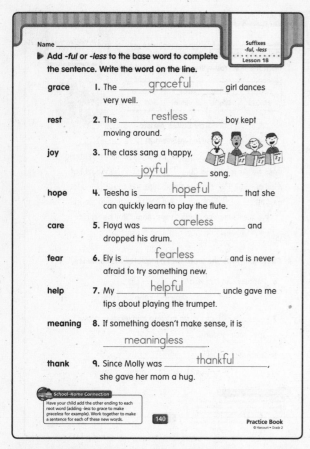

hope   4. Teesha is _____hopeful_____ that she can quickly learn to play the flute.

care   5. Floyd was _____careless_____ and dropped his drum.

fear   6. Ely is _____fearless_____ and is never afraid to try something new.

help   7. My _____helpful_____ uncle gave me tips about playing the trumpet.

meaning   8. If something doesn't make sense, it is _____meaningless_____

thank   9. Since Molly was _____thankful_____, she gave her mom a hug.

School-Home Connection
Have your child add the other ending to each root word (adding *-less* to grace to make *graceless* for example). Work together to make a sentence for each of these new words.

140

Practice Book
© Harcourt • Grade 2

Name _____

▶ Read the sentences. Circle the adjectives that tell how many. Underline the nouns they describe.

1. My brother can play (many) instruments.

2. He has (two) guitars and (one) drum.

3. (One) day he will teach me to play that drum.

▶ Write each sentence, using an adjective that tells how many. **Possible responses are shown.**

4. Jeff walked (how many) miles today.

   Jeff walked three miles today.

5. We spent (how many) hours at the gym.

   We spent two hours at the gym.

6. This book (how many) poems in it.

   This book has many poems in it.

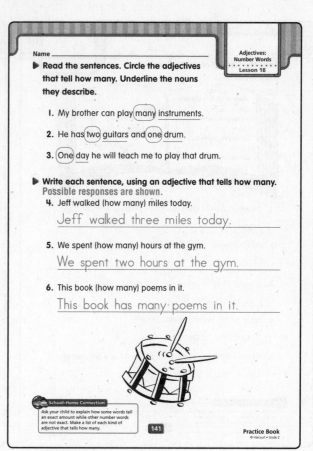

School-Home Connection
Ask your child to explain how some words tell an exact amount while other number words are not exact. Make a list of each kind of adjective that tells how many.

141

Practice Book
© Harcourt • Grade 2

Name _____

▶ Circle the word that completes each sentence.

1. Each _____, Dad's garden starts to bloom.
   early   your   (year)

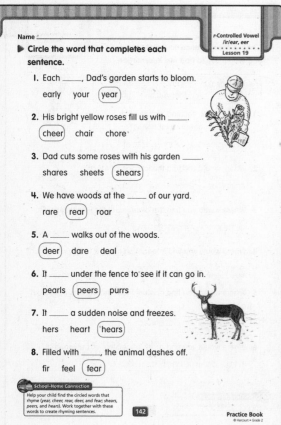

2. His bright yellow roses fill us with _____.
   (cheer)   chair   chore

3. Dad cuts some roses with his garden _____.
   shares   sheets   (shears)

4. We have woods at the _____ of our yard.
   rare   (rear)   roar

5. A _____ walks out of the woods.
   (deer)   dare   deal

6. It _____ under the fence to see if it can go in.
   pearls   (peers)   purrs

7. It _____ a sudden noise and freezes.
   hers   heart   (hears)

8. Filled with _____, the animal dashes off.
   fir   feel   (fear)

School-Home Connection
Help your child find the circled words that rhyme (*year, cheer, rear, deer,* and *fear; shears, peers,* and *hears*). Work together with these words to create rhyming sentences.

142

Practice Book
© Harcourt • Grade 2

Name _____

▶ Read the Spelling Words. Sort them and write them where they belong.
Order may vary.

Words with *ear*

1. gear
2. fear
3. year
4. near
5. hear
6. clear
7. rear

Words Without *ear*

8. deer
9. cheer
10. steer

Spelling Words

gear
deer
fear
year
cheer
near
hear
clear
steer
rear

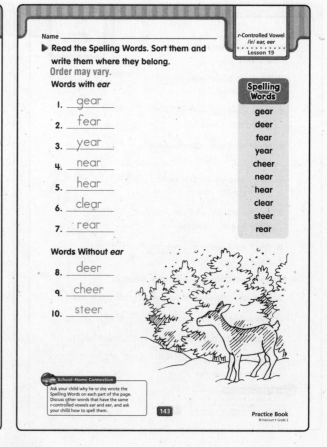

School-Home Connection
Ask your child why he or she wrote the Spelling Words on each part of the page. Discuss other words that have the same *r*-controlled vowels ear and eer, and ask your child how to spell them.

143

Practice Book
© Harcourt • Grade 2

© Harcourt • Grade 2

Student Edition pp. 140–143

Panel 1 (Top Left)

▶ Read the title and headings for a biography about the first female African American millionaire. Then fill in the chart.

Biography of Madame C. J. Walker

Childhood — Daughter of Former Slaves
Early Career — Creating and Selling Hair Products
Middle Career — Training Women to Sell Her Products
Later Career — Starting a Cosmetics Company
Other Achievements — Working for African American Causes

Heading	What does this section tell about?
Childhood	It tells that she was the daughter of former slaves.
Early Career	It tells about her career selling hair products.
Middle Career	It tells about how she trained other women.
Later Career	It tells how she started her own company.
Other Achievements	It tells how she helped African Americans.

School-Home Connection
With your child read a nonfiction book that has headings. Ask him or her to explain why the author chose to include headings and what the headings tell about each section.

144

Practice Book
© Harcourt • Grade 2

Panel 2 (Top Right)

▶ Complete the story. On each line, write a word from the box. You will not use all the words.

clear	fearful	steer
hear	cheerful	year

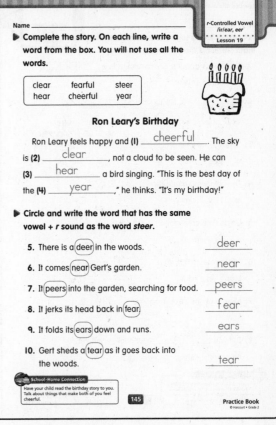

Ron Leary's Birthday

Ron Leary feels happy and (1) __cheerful__. The sky is (2) __clear__, not a cloud to be seen. He can (3) __hear__ a bird singing. "This is the best day of the (4) __year__," he thinks. "It's my birthday!"

▶ Circle and write the word that has the same vowel + r sound as the word *steer*.

5. There is a (deer) in the woods. ___deer___

6. It comes (near) Gert's garden. ___near___

7. It (peers) into the garden, searching for food. ___peers___

8. It jerks its head back in (fear). ___fear___

9. It folds its (ears) down and runs. ___ears___

10. Gert sheds a (tear) as it goes back into the woods. ___tear___

School-Home Connection
Have your child read the birthday story to you. Talk about things that make both of you feel cheerful.

145

Practice Book
© Harcourt • Grade 2

Panel 3 (Bottom Left)

▶ Circle the answer to each question.

1. Which of these are art **supplies**?
(paints and brushes)   red and green   draws and sketches

2. When do you do **experiments** in school?
in art class   in math class   (in science class)

3. What does a worker **earn** each week?
a new task   (money)   the same job

4. What does a **committee** do?
(decides things)   makes meals   plays sports

5. Which of these is a **crop**?
police   (peanuts)   books

6. Which ones **provide** help?
playgrounds   pencils   (teachers)

7. Which of these are school **supplies**?
hammer and nails   (paper and pencil)   floors and walls

8. How do you **earn** a reward?
sleep   cry   (try your best)

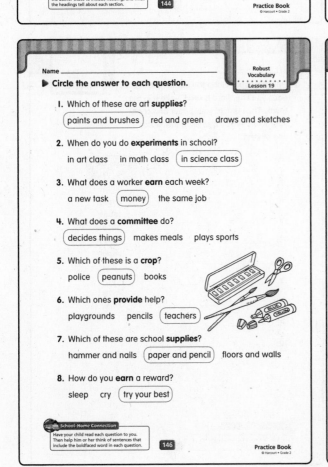

School-Home Connection
Have your child read each question to you. Then help him or her think of sentences that include the boldfaced word in each question.

146

Practice Book
© Harcourt • Grade 2

Panel 4 (Bottom Right)

▶ Write a reference source from the box to answer each question.

encyclopedia	atlas	dictionary	thesaurus

1. Where would you find the most information about the life of Abraham Lincoln? __encyclopedia__

2. Where could you see the location of Australia? __atlas__

3. Where would you find the most information about musical instruments? __encyclopedia__

4. Where would you find another word that means about the same as famous? __thesaurus__

5. Where would you look to learn about the invention of airplanes? __encyclopedia__

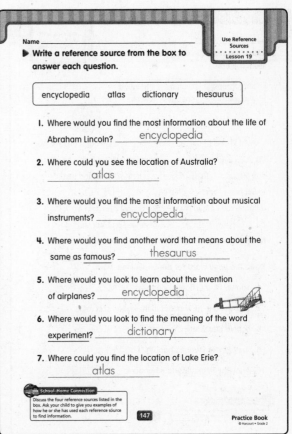

6. Where would you look to find the meaning of the word experiment? __dictionary__

7. Where could you find the location of Lake Erie? __atlas__

School-Home Connection
Discuss the four reference sources listed in the box. Ask your child to give you examples of how he or she has used each reference source to find information.

147

Practice Book
© Harcourt • Grade 2

© Harcourt • Grade 2

▶ **Put two syllables together to make a word that completes the sentence.**

1. This tale is about a prince who rode a _____dragon_____
   on   drag   wag

2. Malik made a _____dozen_____ bran muffins.
   doz   driv   en

3. Silver is one kind of _____metal_____.
   al   ped   met

4. The cold wind made Kim _____shiver_____.
   er   shiv   clev

5. Uncle Pete came for a _____visit_____.
   it   vis   lim

6. Hang your shirt in your _____closet_____.
   plan   et   clos

7. Mom took the cake out of the _____oven_____.
   sev   ov   en

8. Did you _____finish_____ your book report yet?
   fin   van   ish

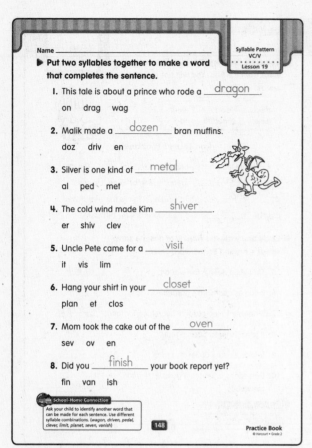

▶ **Read each sentence. Circle the correct adjective in ( ) that completes the sentence.**

1. Mrs. Hardin has the (bigger, biggest) house on our street.

2. Our door is (taller, tallest) than her door.

3. She serves the (sweeter, sweetest) lemonade ever made.

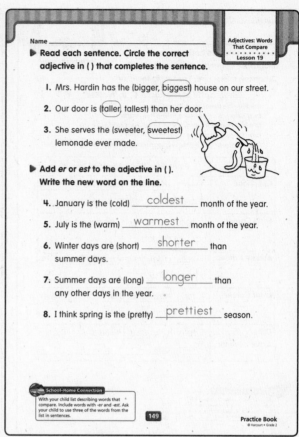

▶ **Add er or est to the adjective in ( ). Write the new word on the line.**

4. January is the (cold) _____coldest_____ month of the year.

5. July is the (warm) _____warmest_____ month of the year.

6. Winter days are (short) _____shorter_____ than summer days.

7. Summer days are (long) _____longer_____ than any other days in the year.

8. I think spring is the (pretty) _____prettiest_____ season.

▶ **Finish the story. On each line, write a word from the box.**

| photograph | knitted | laughed |
| wrapped | enough | wrote |

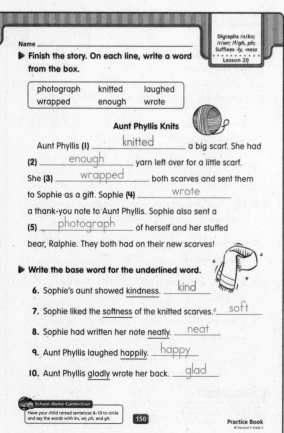

Aunt Phyllis Knits

Aunt Phyllis (1) _____knitted_____ a big scarf. She had

(2) _____enough_____ yarn left over for a little scarf.

She (3) _____wrapped_____ both scarves and sent them

to Sophie as a gift. Sophie (4) _____wrote_____

a thank-you note to Aunt Phyllis. Sophie also sent a

(5) _____photograph_____ of herself and her stuffed

bear, Ralphie. They both had on their new scarves!

▶ **Write the base word for the underlined word.**

6. Sophie's aunt showed kindness. _____kind_____

7. Sophie liked the softness of the knitted scarves. _____soft_____

8. Sophie had written her note neatly. _____neat_____

9. Aunt Phyllis laughed happily. _____happy_____

10. Aunt Phyllis gladly wrote her back. _____glad_____

▶ **Fold the paper along the dotted line. As each Spelling Word is read, write it in the blank. Then unfold your paper and check your work. Practice spelling any words you missed.**

1. _____
2. _____
3. _____
4. _____
5. _____
6. _____
7. _____
8. _____
9. _____
10. _____

Spelling Words

know
wrong
tough
phone
breath
health
soil
joy
deer
rear

Student Edition pp. 148–151

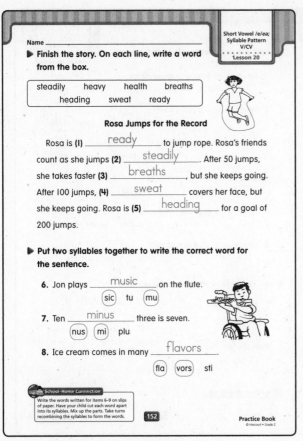

▶ Finish the story. On each line, write a word from the box.

| steadily | heavy | health | breaths |
| heading | sweat | ready | |

Rosa Jumps for the Record

Rosa is **(1)** _____ready_____ to jump rope. Rosa's friends

count as she jumps **(2)** _____steadily_____. After 50 jumps,

she takes faster **(3)** _____breaths_____, but she keeps going.

After 100 jumps, **(4)** _____sweat_____ covers her face, but

she keeps going. Rosa is **(5)** _____heading_____ for a goal of

200 jumps.

▶ Put two syllables together to write the correct word for the sentence.

6. Jon plays _____music_____ on the flute.
   (sic) tu (mu)

7. Ten _____minus_____ three is seven.
   (nus) (mi) plu

8. Ice cream comes in many _____flavors_____
   (fla) (vors) sti

School-Home Connection
Write the words written for items 6–9 on slips of paper. Have your child cut each word apart into its syllables. Mix up the parts. Take turns recombining the syllables to form the words.

152

Practice Book
© Harcourt • Grade 2

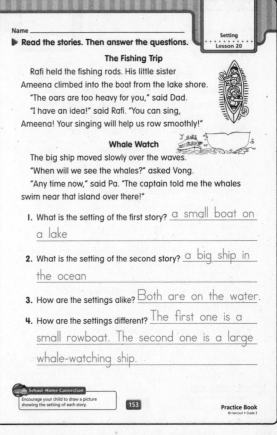

▶ Read the stories. Then answer the questions.

The Fishing Trip

Rafi held the fishing rods. His little sister
Ameena climbed into the boat from the lake shore.

"The oars are too heavy for you," said Dad.

"I have an idea!" said Rafi. "You can sing,
Ameena! Your singing will help us row smoothly!"

Whale Watch

The big ship moved slowly over the waves.

"When will we see the whales?" asked Vong.

"Any time now," said Pa. "The captain told me the whales
swim near that island over there!"

1. What is the setting of the first story? a small boat on a lake

2. What is the setting of the second story? a big ship in the ocean

3. How are the settings alike? Both are on the water.

4. How are the settings different? The first one is a small rowboat. The second one is a large whale-watching ship.

School-Home Connection
Encourage your child to draw a picture showing the setting of each story.

153

Practice Book
© Harcourt • Grade 2

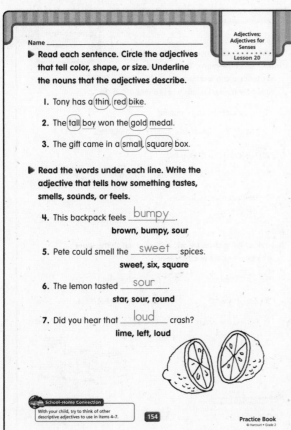

▶ Read each sentence. Circle the adjectives that tell color, shape, or size. Underline the nouns that the adjectives describe.

1. Tony has a (thin), (red) bike.

2. The (tall) boy won the (gold) medal.

3. The gift came in a (small), (square) box.

▶ Read the words under each line. Write the adjective that tells how something tastes, smells, sounds, or feels.

4. This backpack feels _____bumpy_____
   brown, bumpy, sour

5. Pete could smell the _____sweet_____ spices.
   sweet, six, square

6. The lemon tasted _____sour_____.
   star, sour, round

7. Did you hear that _____loud_____ crash?
   lime, left, loud

School-Home Connection
With your child, try to think of other descriptive adjectives to use in items 4–7.

154

Practice Book
© Harcourt • Grade 2

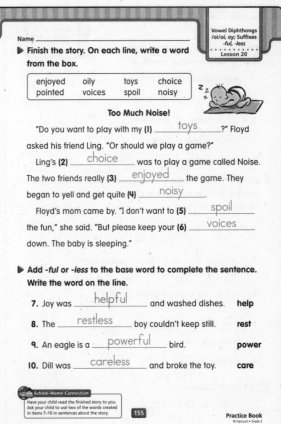

▶ Finish the story. On each line, write a word from the box.

| enjoyed | oily | toys | choice |
| pointed | voices | spoil | noisy |

Too Much Noise!

"Do you want to play with my **(1)** _____toys_____?" Floyd

asked his friend Ling. "Or should we play a game?"

Ling's **(2)** _____choice_____ was to play a game called Noise.

The two friends really **(3)** _____enjoyed_____ the game. They

began to yell and get quite **(4)** _____noisy_____.

Floyd's mom came by. "I don't want to **(5)** _____spoil_____

the fun," she said. "But please keep your **(6)** _____voices_____

down. The baby is sleeping."

▶ Add -ful or -less to the base word to complete the sentence. Write the word on the line.

7. Joy was _____helpful_____ and washed dishes. **help**

8. The _____restless_____ boy couldn't keep still. **rest**

9. An eagle is a _____powerful_____ bird. **power**

10. Dill was _____careless_____ and broke the toy. **care**

School-Home Connection
Have your child read the finished story to you. Ask your child to use two of the words created in items 7–10 in sentences about the story.

155

Practice Book
© Harcourt • Grade 2

▶ **Read the directions. Then answer the questions.**

How to Make a Paperweight

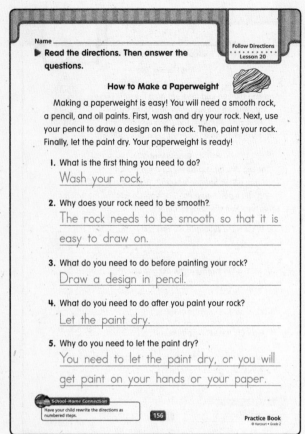

Making a paperweight is easy! You will need a smooth rock, a pencil, and oil paints. First, wash and dry your rock. Next, use your pencil to draw a design on the rock. Then, paint your rock. Finally, let the paint dry. Your paperweight is ready!

1. What is the first thing you need to do?

Wash your rock.

2. Why does your rock need to be smooth?

The rock needs to be smooth so that it is easy to draw on.

3. What do you need to do before painting your rock?

Draw a design in pencil.

4. What do you need to do after you paint your rock?

Let the paint dry.

5. Why do you need to let the paint dry?

You need to let the paint dry, or you will get paint on your hands or your paper.

School-Home Connection
Have your child rewrite the directions as numbered steps.

156

Practice Book
© Harcourt • Grade 2

▶ **Write the word that answers the question.**

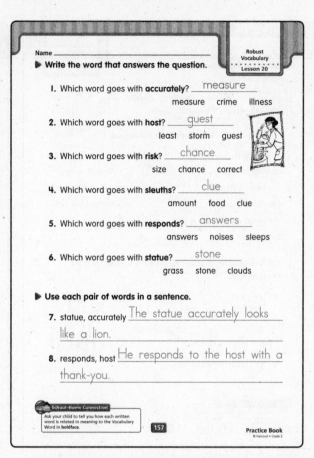

1. Which word goes with **accurately**? __measure__

   measure   crime   illness

2. Which word goes with **host**? __guest__

   least   storm   guest

3. Which word goes with **risk**? __chance__

   size   chance   correct

4. Which word goes with **sleuths**? __clue__

   amount   food   clue

5. Which word goes with **responds**? __answers__

   answers   noises   sleeps

6. Which word goes with **statue**? __stone__

   grass   stone   clouds

▶ **Use each pair of words in a sentence.**

7. statue, accurately   The statue accurately looks like a lion.

8. responds, host   He responds to the host with a thank-you.

School-Home Connection
Ask your child to tell you how each written word is related in meaning to the Vocabulary Word in **boldface**.

157

Practice Book
© Harcourt • Grade 2

▶ **Circle and write the word that has the same vowel + r sound as the word** *here.*

1. There are woods (near) Cal's home. __near__

2. Cal searches for (deer) in the woods. __deer__

3. Cal (peers) closely at some ferns. __peers__

4. He (hears) a bird up in a fir tree. __hears__

5. He likes her (cheerful) song. __cheerful__

▶ **Below each sentence are three syllables. Put two syllables together to make a word that completes the sentence. Write the word on the line.**

6. We live on the __planet__ called Earth.

   (et)   clos   (plan)

7. A __lizard__ and a snake are both reptiles.

   tur   (liz)   (ard)

8. Hana put her foot on the bike __pedal__.

   lev   (al)   (ped)

9. A __robin__ perched on the tree branch.

   (rob)   jay   (in)

10. Grandma likes __lemon__ in her tea.

    (on)   wag   (lem)

School-Home Connection
Have your child write five new sentences. Each sentence should use one of the answer words from items 1–5 and one of the answer words from items 6–10.

158

Practice Book
© Harcourt • Grade 2

▶ **Read each sentence. Circle the adjective that tells how many. Then write a new sentence using a different adjective that tells how many. Possible responses are shown.**

1. (Five) children went camping.

   Twelve children went camping.

2. (Two) adults went with them.

   Five adults went with them.

3. They saw (many) animals.

   They saw ten animals.

▶ **Look at the picture below. Add er or est to the word in ( ) to complete each sentence.**

4. Pot 2 is (big) __bigger__ than Pot 1.

5. Pot 1 is (wide) __wider__ than Pot 3.

6. Pot 1 is the (short) __shortest__.

7. Pot 3 is the (tall) __tallest__.

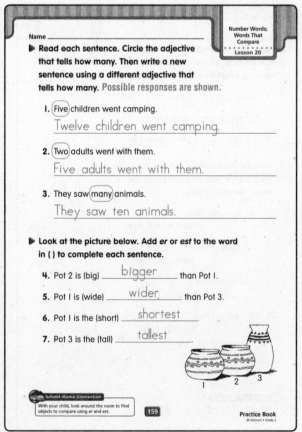

1   2   3

School-Home Connection
With your child, look around the room to find objects to compare using er and est.

159

Practice Book
© Harcourt • Grade 2

Student Edition pp. 156–159

Locate Information
Lesson 20

▶ Read the table of contents. Then answer the questions.

A Famous Inventor: Thomas Edison

1. Which chapter tells about Thomas Edison's childhood?
   Chapter 1

2. Which page would tell how Thomas Edison invented the light bulb?
   page 19

3. Which chapter would tell about the invention of the phonograph?
   Chapter 4

4. Where might you look to find the meaning of the words **telegraph** and **phonograph**?
   the Glossary, page 30

5. What kind of information might you find in Chapter 2?
   how Thomas Edison worked as a telegraph operator

School-Home Connection
Have your child use the table of contents to tell you what this book could tell him or her about Thomas Edison.

160

Practice Book
© Harcourt • Grade 2

Use References Sources
Lesson 20

▶ Write the name of a reference source from the box to answer each question.

| encyclopedia | atlas | map |
| dictionary | thesaurus | |

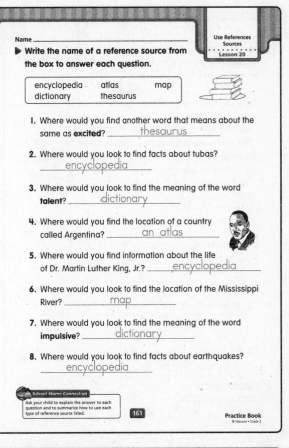

1. Where would you find another word that means about the same as **excited**? thesaurus

2. Where would you look to find facts about tubas? encyclopedia

3. Where would you look to find the meaning of the word **talent**? dictionary

4. Where would you find the location of a country called Argentina? an atlas

5. Where would you find information about the life of Dr. Martin Luther King, Jr.? encyclopedia

6. Where would you look to find the location of the Mississippi River? map

7. Where would you look to find the meaning of the word **impulsive**? dictionary

8. Where would you look to find facts about earthquakes? encyclopedia

School-Home Connection
Ask your child to explain the answer to each question and to summarize how to use each type of reference source listed.

161

Practice Book
© Harcourt • Grade 2

Vowel Diphthong /ou/ou, ow
Lesson 21

▶ Underline the word that goes with each picture.

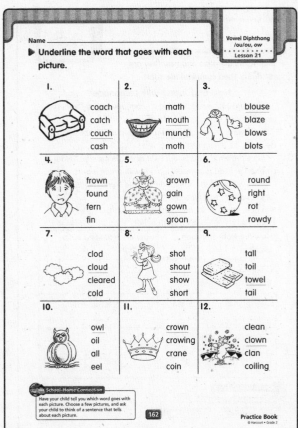

1. coach / catch / couch / cash
2. math / mouth / munch / moth
3. blouse / blaze / blows / blots
4. frown / found / fern / fin
5. grown / gain / gown / groan
6. round / right / rot / rowdy
7. clod / cloud / cleared / cold
8. shot / shout / show / short
9. tall / toil / towel / tail
10. owl / oil / all / eel
11. crown / crowing / crane / coin
12. clean / clown / clan / coiling

School-Home Connection
Have your child tell you which word goes with each picture. Choose a few pictures, and ask your child to think of a sentence that tells about each picture.

162

Practice Book
© Harcourt • Grade 2

Vowel Diphthongs /ou/ ou, ow
Lesson 21

▶ Read the Spelling Words. Sort them and write them where they belong.

Words with _ou_

1. out
2. count
3. ground
4. found
5. sound

Words with _ow_

6. town
7. crowd
8. now
9. crown
10. down

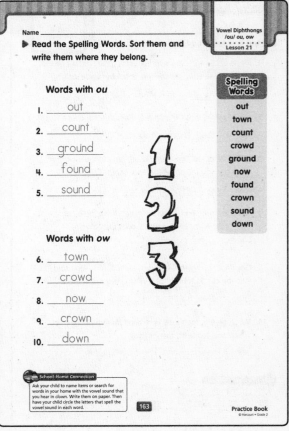

Spelling Words

out
town
count
crowd
ground
now
found
crown
sound
down

School-Home Connection
Ask your child to name items or search for words in your home with the vowel sound you hear in clown. Write them on paper. Then have your child circle the letters that spell the vowel sound in each word.

163

Practice Book
© Harcourt • Grade 2

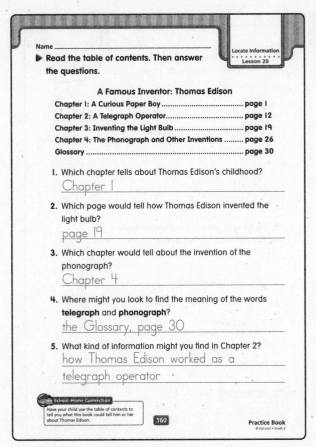

Name _____

▶ Read the story and fill in the chart.
Tell about the problem, the important events, and the solution to the problem.

A Whole New Bike

"I want a bike," said Tim. "But I don't have enough money."

"Mrs. Ball needs help walking her dogs," said Mom. "She might give you a job."

Tim went to see Mrs. Ball. He walked her dogs all summer long. At the end of the summer, Mom helped Tim count his money.

"It's enough for a bike!" said Mom.

Mom smiled and said, "You've worked hard and I am proud of you."

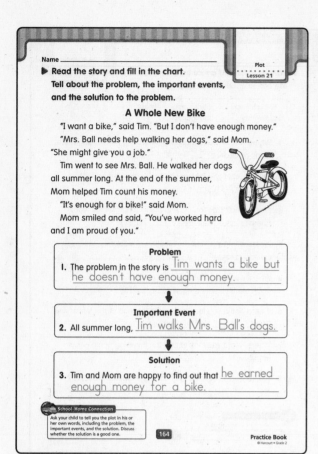

Problem
1. The problem in the story is Tim wants a bike but he doesn't have enough money.

Important Event
2. All summer long, Tim walks Mrs. Ball's dogs.

Solution
3. Tim and Mom are happy to find out that he earned enough money for a bike.

School-Home Connection
Ask your child to tell you the plot in his or her own words, including the problem, the important events, and the solution. Discuss whether the solution is a good one.

164

Name _____

▶ Write each word from the box under the word that has the same vowel sound.

count	crowd	bowl
thrown	soak	sound

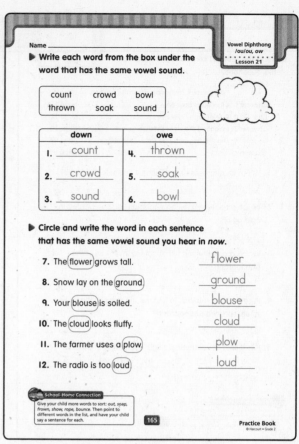

down		owe	
1. count		4. thrown	
2. crowd		5. soak	
3. sound		6. bowl	

▶ Circle and write the word in each sentence that has the same vowel sound you hear in *now*.

7. The (flower) grows tall. flower

8. Snow lay on the (ground). ground

9. Your (blouse) is soiled. blouse

10. The (cloud) looks fluffy. cloud

11. The farmer uses a (plow). plow

12. The radio is too (loud). loud

School-Home Connection
Give your child more words to sort: *out, soap, frown, show, rope, bounce.* Then point to different words in the list, and have your child say a sentence for each.

165

Name _____

▶ Read and answer each question.

1. Marie exchanged the shirt her uncle gave her for one that was smaller. How did she feel about her uncle's gift?

She liked the gift, but it didn't fit.

2. Mom can tell that the milk is spoiled. What should she do?

She should throw it away

3. Most CDs at Hot Spot cost $12.00. Jerry found a bargain. What can you tell about the price of his CD?

It is less than $12.00.

4. The band marched down the street. "Give me a boost, Dad," said Woody. What was Woody's problem?

He couldn't see the band.

5. One chair was metal. One was stuffed. Mrs. Alba said, "I'll take the comfortable chair." Which chair did she choose?

She chose the stuffed chair.

6. Mr. Steen has meals delivered and Mr. Breen does not. Which one cooks his own meals?

Mr. Breen cooks his own meals.

School-Home Connection
Ask your child to explain the reasoning behind each written response. For example, how did your child figure out that Marie liked her uncle's gift even though she exchanged it?

166

Name _____

▶ Read the story. Think about how the characters are alike and how they are different. Then complete the chart.

Noel and Juan Make Lemonade

Noel and Juan were opening a lemonade stand. They liked to work together.

"I will write the word LEMONADE," said Juan. "I like writing." He wrote the letters neatly on a sign.

"I like drawing," said Noel. "I will decorate the sign." Noel carefully painted four yellow lemons with green leaves.

"Who will make the lemonade?" asked Mom.

"Both of us!" said Noel and Juan together. "We both like to make and drink lemonade!"

Possible responses are shown below.

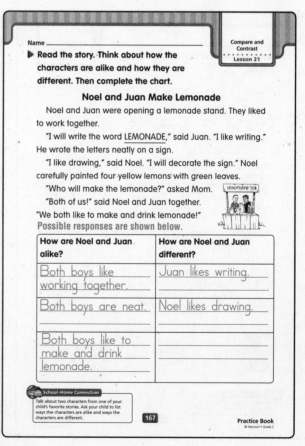

How are Noel and Juan alike?	How are Noel and Juan different?
Both boys like working together.	Juan likes writing.
Both boys are neat.	Noel likes drawing.
Both boys like to make and drink lemonade.	

School-Home Connection
Talk about two characters from one of your child's favorite stories. Ask your child to list ways the characters are alike and ways the characters are different.

167

Abbreviations
Lesson 21

► A word is underlined in each sentence. On the line, write the abbreviation for the underlined word.

1. Thanksgiving is in November.   Nov.
2. I went to the movies last Sunday.   Sun.
3. We have a math test on Wednesday.   Wed.
4. We go on vacation in August.   Aug.
5. Esther's dad is Mister Valdez.   Mr.
6. Jamal's mom is Doctor Kanza.   Dr.
7. Zeke's birthday is October 7.   Oct.
8. Mom always travels for work in April.   Apr.
9. We will go shopping on Saturday.   Sat.
10. Sam has football practice on Tuesday.   Tues.
11. Valentine's Day is in February.   Feb.
12. Fall begins in September.   Sept.

School-Home Connection
Use a calendar to find the dates (months and days) of important family events. Have your child list them, using the proper abbreviations.

168

Practice Book
© Harcourt • Grade 2

Present-Tense
Action Verbs
Lesson 21

► Complete each sentence by adding a verb. Look at the picture for ideas.
Possible responses are shown.

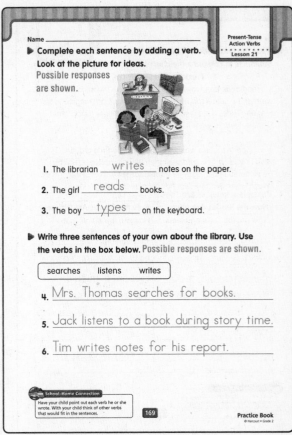

1. The librarian _writes_ notes on the paper.
2. The girl _reads_ books.
3. The boy _types_ on the keyboard.

► Write three sentences of your own about the library. Use the verbs in the box below. Possible responses are shown.

| searches | listens | writes |

4. Mrs. Thomas searches for books.
5. Jack listens to a book during story time.
6. Tim writes notes for his report.

School-Home Connection
Have your child point out each verb he or she wrote. With your child think of other verbs that would fit in the sentences.

169

Practice Book
© Harcourt • Grade 2

---

r-Controlled Vowel
/ôr/or, ore, our
Lesson 22

► Circle the word that completes each sentence.

1. Mort has many _____ to do around the farm.
    chairs   (chores)   chose

2. He feeds hay to all his _____.
    (horses)   hoses   houses

3. He feeds _____ to his forty hens.
    cone   core   (corn)

4. He gets more feed from the corner _____.
    star   storm   (store)

5. He works hard every day until _____ o'clock.
    (four)   for   fur

6. Then he sits on his front _____ and rests.
    pouch   (porch)   pours

7. He _____ himself some cold water.
    ports   pores   (pours)

8. Then he takes a nap and _____.
    (snores)   snare   shores

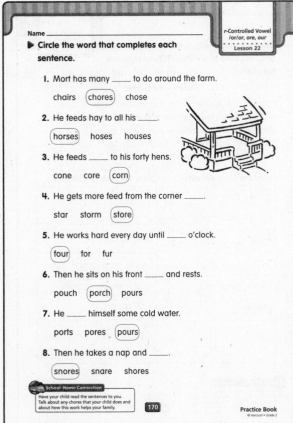

School-Home Connection
Have your child read the sentences to you. Talk about any chores that your child does and about how this work helps your family.

170

Practice Book
© Harcourt • Grade 2

---

r-Controlled
Vowels /ôr/or,
ore, our
Lesson 22

► Read the Spelling Words. Sort them and write them where they belong.

Words with *ore*	Words with *or*
1. store	6. fork
2. score	7. short
3. chore	
4. more	
5. sore	

Words with *our*

8. pour
9. your
10. four

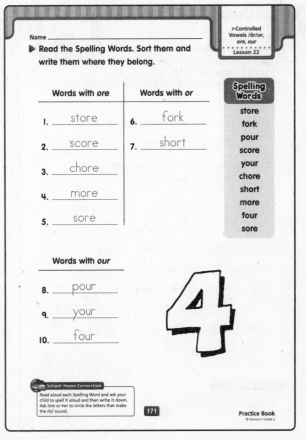

Spelling Words
store
fork
pour
score
your
chore
short
more
four
sore

School-Home Connection
Read aloud each Spelling Word and ask your child to spell it aloud and then write it down. Ask him or her to circle the letters that make the /ôr/ sound.

171

Practice Book
© Harcourt • Grade 2

© Harcourt • Grade 2

45

Student Edition pp. 168–171

▶ Read the two stories. Then answer the questions to complete the chart.

Freddie Tries a Worm

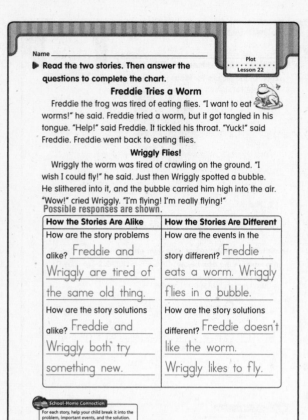

Freddie the frog was tired of eating flies. "I want to eat worms!" he said. Freddie tried a worm, but it got tangled in his tongue. "Help!" said Freddie. It tickled his throat. "Yuck!" said Freddie. Freddie went back to eating flies.

Wriggly Flies!

Wriggly the worm was tired of crawling on the ground. "I wish I could fly!" he said. Just then Wriggly spotted a bubble. He slithered into it, and the bubble carried him high into the air. "Wow!" cried Wriggly. "I'm flying! I'm really flying!"

Possible responses are shown.

How the Stories Are Alike	How the Stories Are Different
How are the story problems alike? Freddie and Wriggly are tired of the same old thing.	How are the events in the story different? Freddie eats a worm. Wriggly flies in a bubble.
How are the story solutions alike? Freddie and Wriggly both try something new.	How are the story solutions different? Freddie doesn't like the worm. Wriggly likes to fly.

School-Home Connection
For each story, help your child break it into the problem, important events, and the solution. Then discuss how the stories are alike and how they are different.

172

Practice Book
© Harcourt • Grade 2

▶ Finish the story. Write a word from the box on each line.

sports	chores	four	morning	more
score	pour	boring	short	wore

Uncle Frank's Farm

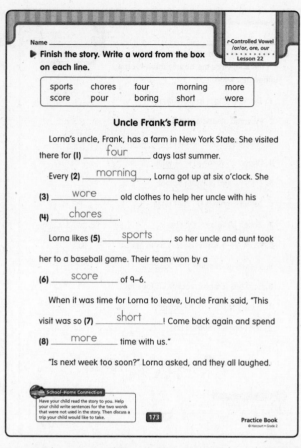

Lorna's uncle, Frank, has a farm in New York State. She visited there for **(1)** _____four_____ days last summer.

Every **(2)** _____morning_____, Lorna got up at six o'clock. She

(3) _____wore_____ old clothes to help her uncle with his

(4) _____chores_____.

Lorna likes **(5)** _____sports_____, so her uncle and aunt took her to a baseball game. Their team won by a

(6) _____score_____ of 9–6.

When it was time for Lorna to leave, Uncle Frank said, "This

visit was so **(7)** _____short_____! Come back again and spend

(8) _____more_____ time with us."

"Is next week too soon?" Lorna asked, and they all laughed.

School-Home Connection
Have your child read the story to you. Help your child write sentences for the two words that were not used in the story. Then discuss a trip your child would like to take.

173

Practice Book
© Harcourt • Grade 2

▶ Answer each question with *Yes* or *No*. Tell why you gave that answer.

Possible responses are shown.

1. If you're barely awake, are you not at all sleepy?
   No. You are feeling sleepy.

2. If you admit something, do you keep it secret?
   No. You tell something if you admit it.

3. Should you see a doctor if you're extremely sick?
   Yes. You need to see a doctor.

4. Would you worry if you made a serious mistake?
   Yes. I would be upset.

5. Would you laugh if a cartoon were hilarious?
   Yes. I would laugh a lot.

6. Does a witty person tell good jokes?
   Yes. A witty person is clever and funny.

7. Would you laugh a lot if a joke was barely funny?
   No. You would not laugh.

School-Home Connection
Read each question, and have your child read the response on the lines. Use questions 5–7 to talk about what makes you both laugh. Share funny jokes each of you has heard.

174

Practice Book
© Harcourt • Grade 2

▶ Read the paragraph. Think about how the birds are alike and different. Then complete the chart.

Ducks and Geese

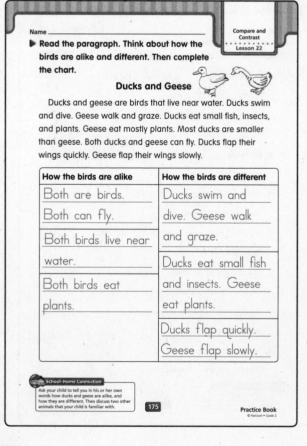

Ducks and geese are birds that live near water. Ducks swim and dive. Geese walk and graze. Ducks eat small fish, insects, and plants. Geese eat mostly plants. Most ducks are smaller than geese. Both ducks and geese can fly. Ducks flap their wings quickly. Geese flap their wings slowly.

How the birds are alike	How the birds are different
Both are birds. Both can fly. Both birds live near water. Both birds eat plants.	Ducks swim and dive. Geese walk and graze. Ducks eat small fish and insects. Geese eat plants. Ducks flap quickly. Geese flap slowly.

School-Home Connection
Ask your child to tell you in his or her own words how ducks and geese are alike, and how they are different. Then discuss two other animals that your child is familiar with.

175

Practice Book
© Harcourt • Grade 2

© Harcourt • Grade 2

Student Edition pp. 172–175

Name _____

▶ Underline the two-syllable word in each sentence.

1. Please don't pick that <u>tulip</u>!

2. Ruth is sick and has a <u>fever</u>.

3. Abe lived in a log <u>cabin</u>.

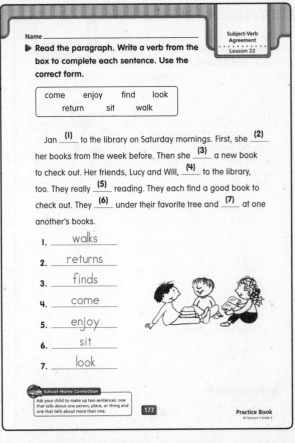

4. A <u>pilot</u> flies a plane.

5. Did you put <u>lemon</u> in my tea?

6. A boat went down the <u>river</u>.

7. The <u>spider</u> spun a web.

8. It is best to keep your <u>promise</u>.

▶ Write each underlined word in the column with the same syllable pattern.

meter (V/CV)	metal (VC/V)
9. tulip	10. cabin
11. fever	12. lemon
13. pilot	14. river
15. spider	16. promise

School-Home Connection
Ask your child to copy each word from the two lists. Then have your child use a slash mark to divide each listed word into two syllables.

176

Practice Book
© Harcourt • Grade 2

Name _____

▶ Read the paragraph. Write a verb from the box to complete each sentence. Use the correct form.

come	enjoy	find	look
return	sit	walk	

Jan __(1)__ to the library on Saturday mornings. First, she __(2)__ her books from the week before. Then she __(3)__ a new book to check out. Her friends, Lucy and Will, __(4)__ to the library, too. They really __(5)__ reading. They each find a good book to check out. They __(6)__ under their favorite tree and __(7)__ at one another's books.

1. walks

2. returns

3. finds

4. come

5. enjoy

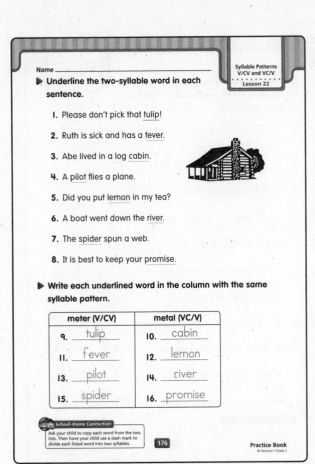

6. sit

7. look

School-Home Connection
Ask your child to make up two sentences: one that tells about one person, place, or thing and one that tells about more than one.

177

Practice Book
© Harcourt • Grade 2

Name _____

▶ Circle the word that goes with each picture.

1. (food) clues few	2. mood moose (moon)	3. soon (soup) spoon
4. knew (threw) pool	5. (loose) scoop blue	6. (flew) spool drew
7. (suit) stew chew	8. stool (boots) smooth	9. bloom blew (broom)
10. true jewels (juice)	11. (glue) grew group	12. smooth (boost) (fruit)

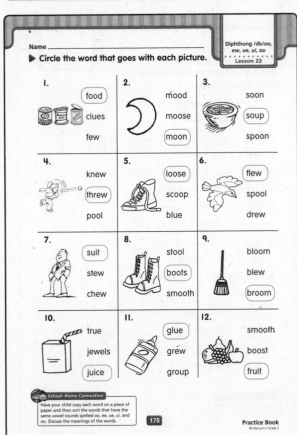

School-Home Connection
Have your child copy each word on a piece of paper and then sort the words that have the same vowel sounds spelled oo, ee, ue, ui, and ou. Discuss the meanings of the words.

178

Practice Book
© Harcourt • Grade 2

Name _____

▶ Make cards for the Spelling Words. Lay them down and read them.

1. Put the words with *oo* in a group. Write them on the chart.

2. Put the words with *ew* in a group. Write them on the chart.

3. Put the words with *ue* in a group. Write them on the chart.

Words with *oo*	Words with *ew*
1. smooth	3. grew
2. food	4. stew

Words with *ue*	
5. true	
6. clue	

▶ Write the words that are left.

7. suit   9. group

8. soup   10. fruit

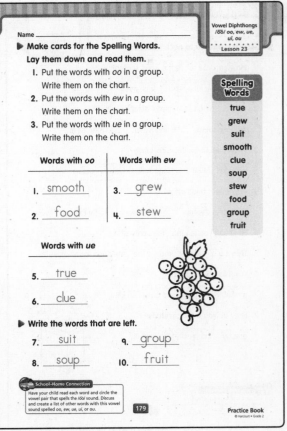

Spelling Words

true
grew
suit
smooth
clue
soup
stew
food
group
fruit

School-Home Connection
Have your child read each word and circle the vowel pair that spells the /ōō/ sound. Discuss and create a list of other words with this vowel sound spelled oo, ew, ue, ui, or ou.

179

Practice Book
© Harcourt • Grade 2

© Harcourt • Grade 2

Student Edition pp. 176–179

Panel 1 (page 180)

Name _____

Use Graphic Aids — Lesson 23

▶ **Read the paragraph. Then use the diagram to answer the questions.**

Ladybugs

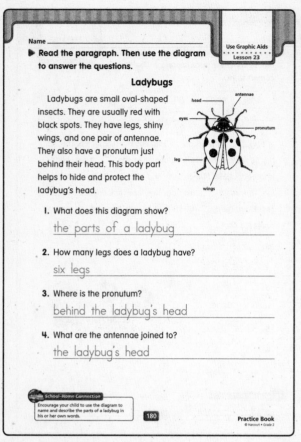

Ladybugs are small oval-shaped insects. They are usually red with black spots. They have legs, shiny wings, and one pair of antennae. They also have a pronutum just behind their head. This body part helps to hide and protect the ladybug's head.

1. What does this diagram show?

   the parts of a ladybug

2. How many legs does a ladybug have?

   six legs

3. Where is the pronutum?

   behind the ladybug's head

4. What are the antennae joined to?

   the ladybug's head

School-Home Connection
Encourage your child to use the diagram to name and describe the parts of a ladybug in his or her own words.

180

Practice Book
© Harcourt • Grade 2

Panel 2 (page 181)

Name _____

Vowel Diphthong /ōō/oo, ew, ue, ui, ou — Lesson 23

▶ **Circle the word in each sentence that has the same vowel sound as *zoo*. Write the word on the line.**

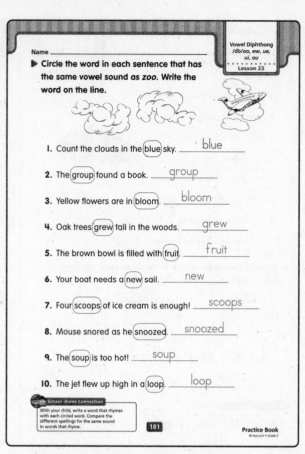

1. Count the clouds in the blue sky. ___blue___

2. The group found a book. ___group___

3. Yellow flowers are in bloom. ___bloom___

4. Oak trees grew tall in the woods. ___grew___

5. The brown bowl is filled with fruit. ___fruit___

6. Your boat needs a new sail. ___new___

7. Four scoops of ice cream is enough! ___scoops___

8. Mouse snored as he snoozed. ___snoozed___

9. The soup is too hot! ___soup___

10. The jet flew up high in a loop. ___loop___

School-Home Connection
With your child, write a word that rhymes with each circled word. Compare the different spellings for the same sound in words that rhyme.

181

Practice Book
© Harcourt • Grade 2

Panel 3 (page 182)

Name _____

Robust Vocabulary — Lesson 23

▶ **Circle the answer to each question.**

1. How can you tell that a jar is **sealed**?

   It is open.   (It is shut.)   It is glass.

2. Why do things sometimes **disappear**?

   (We lose them.)   We find them.   We hear them.

3. What should be done **carefully**?

   eating a snack   spilling milk   (mixing paints)

4. Why might bees **attack**?

   (to protect the hive)   to find flowers   to fly to each other

5. How can you tell that bees **crowd**?

   They buzz.   They sting.   (They are close together.)

6. What forms a **pattern**?

   (a beehive)   bees and ants   a sting

7. How do you work **carefully**?

   quickly   (correctly)   playfully

School-Home Connection
Ask your child to use all of the Vocabulary Words, which are in bold type in the questions, to tell about bees or other insects.

182

Practice Book
© Harcourt • Grade 2

Panel 4 (page 183)

Name _____

Synonyms — Lesson 23

▶ **Read the sentences. Circle the word that is a synonym for the underlined word in the sentence.**

1. Some cells in a comb hold honey.

   save   feel   (contain)

2. Bees crowd around their queen.

   play   (gather)   dance

3. The dog guards the house.

   (protects)   chews   likes

4. The cat searched for the mouse.

   smelled   chased   (looked)

5. The birds will leave in autumn.

   spring   (fall)   summer

6. Suddenly the clouds disappeared.

   danced   bounced   (vanished)

7. The weather was extremely cold.

   barely   famously   (very)

8. He played the role of a teacher.

   song   (part)   desk

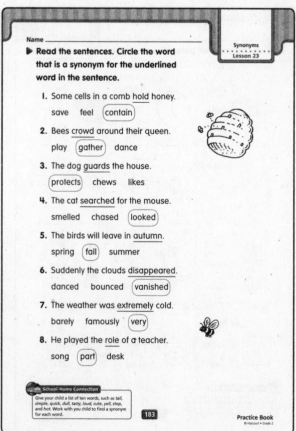

School-Home Connection
Give your child a list of ten words, such as *tall, simple, quick, dull, tasty, loud, cute, yell, stop, and hot*. Work with your child to find a synonym for each word.

183

Practice Book
© Harcourt • Grade 2

© Harcourt • Grade 2

48

***Student Edition* pp. 180–183**

Name _____

▶ Write the prefix from the box that completes the word.

| mis- | re- | un- |

1. I __mis__ spelled the word once, but since then I have always spelled it right.

2. If you tie your laces too tightly, they will be hard to __un__ tie.

3. I __mis__ understood the directions, and did it wrong.

4. If you fill a glass with milk again, you __re__ fill the glass.

5. Always treat a pet well, and never __mis__ treat it.

6. Write your story, and then __re__ write it to make it even better.

7. If we want to play the song again, we can __re__ play it.

8. Bees are like ants in some ways, but they are __un__ like ants in many other ways.

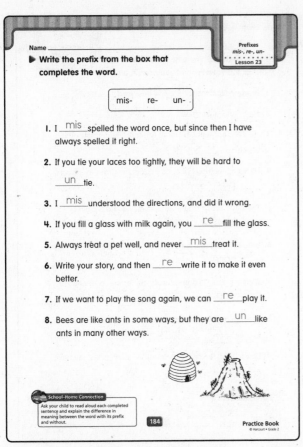

Name _____

▶ Look at the verb in ( ). On the line, write the past-tense form of the verb.

1. Mary (open) __opened__ the door to the store.

2. She (push) __pushed__ the cart down the lanes.

3. Colin (pick) __picked__ his favorite cereal.

4. The store clerk (clean) __cleaned__ up the spill.

5. The cashier (count) __counted__ the money.

6. Sharon (call) __called__ the manager.

7. The manager (check) __checked__ the store to make sure it was clean.

8. The store (close) __closed__ at 10 PM.

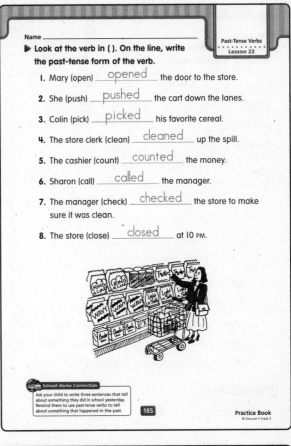

Name _____

▶ Write the word from the box that completes each sentence.

chair	pair	share
stared	scared	hairy
prepare	stairway	care

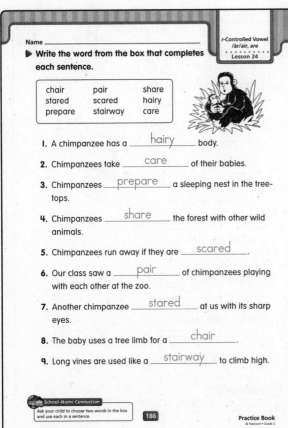

1. A chimpanzee has a __hairy__ body.

2. Chimpanzees take __care__ of their babies.

3. Chimpanzees __prepare__ a sleeping nest in the tree-tops.

4. Chimpanzees __share__ the forest with other wild animals.

5. Chimpanzees run away if they are __scared__.

6. Our class saw a __pair__ of chimpanzees playing with each other at the zoo.

7. Another chimpanzee __stared__ at us with its sharp eyes.

8. The baby uses a tree limb for a __chair__.

9. Long vines are used like a __stairway__ to climb high.

Name _____

▶ Read the Spelling Words. Sort them and write them where they belong.

Words with *air*	Words with *are*
1. hair	6. glare
2. fair	7. scare
3. pair	8. care
4. chair	9. share
5. stair	10. rare

Spelling Words

hair
glare
fair
scare
pair
care
share
chair
rare
stair

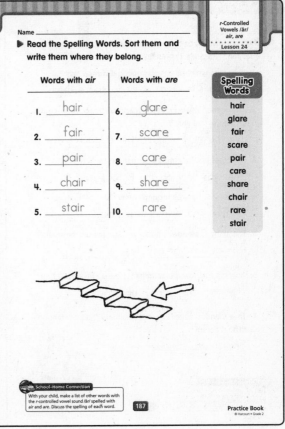

Panel 1 (top left)

Name _____

▶ Read the information in the chart. Then use the chart to answer the questions.

	Chimps	Gorillas
Weight	70–130 pounds	150–500 pounds
Fur Color	black; light or dark brown	black or brownish-gray
Habitat	Africa	Africa
Diet	plants, insects, birds, small mammals	plants, roots, fungi, insects

1. How much do chimps weigh? _Chimps weigh 70-130 pounds._

2. Which animals weigh more, chimps or gorillas? _Gorillas weigh more._

3. Where do chimps and gorillas live? _Chimps and gorillas live in Africa._

4. How are chimps and gorillas' diets alike and different? _Chimps and gorillas both eat plants and insects, but chimps also eat animals._

Panel 2 (top right)

Name _____

▶ In each sentence, circle and write the word that has the vowel sound you hear in *air*.

1. Bradley sits on a (chair) in the backyard. _chair_

2. He is (careful) to sit very still. _careful_

3. He does not want to startle or (scare) the animals he is watching. _scare_

4. He watches a (pair) of birds peck in the grass for insects. _pair_

5. The birds are finding insects near the porch (stairs). _stairs_

6. Bradley can see a (hare) sitting in the shade under a tree. _hare_

7. A young squirrel gathers nuts to (prepare) for winter. _prepare_

8. The squirrel darts away when it sees that Bradley has no food to (share). _share_

9. When Bradley sits, and (stares,) he learns about animals. _stares_

Panel 3 (bottom left)

Name _____

▶ Use your own ideas to answer each question. Possible responses are shown.

1. A woman watched animals from a **distance**. Why? _Maybe she didn't want to scare them._

2. The woman wrote notes on **crumpled** paper. How did the paper get that way? _Maybe it was stuffed in a pocket._

3. A mother animal **cradled** her baby in her lap. Why? _She was keeping the baby safe._

4. An animal's fur was **raggedy**. How did it get that way? _Maybe the animal was sick._

5. The animals **blended** into the forest. How did they look? _They were hard to see._

6. Animals can have **personalities**. How do they show that? _They act shy, funny, or brave._

7. They **blended** sugar into the lemonade. Did the lemonade taste different? _Yes. It was sweeter._

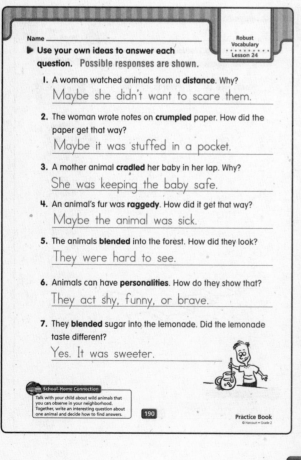

Panel 4 (bottom right)

Name _____

▶ Read each sentence. Circle the synonym for the underlined word.

1. When my team lost, I felt <u>discouraged</u>.
   happy   tired   (disappointed)

2. Dad picked up the <u>crumpled</u> newspaper.
   interesting   heavy   (crushed)

3. The rooster crowed at <u>dawn</u>.
   (sunrise)   sunset   night

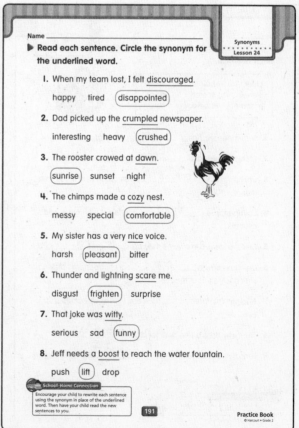

4. The chimps made a <u>cozy</u> nest.
   messy   special   (comfortable)

5. My sister has a very <u>nice</u> voice.
   harsh   (pleasant)   bitter

6. Thunder and lightning <u>scare</u> me.
   disgust   (frighten)   surprise

7. That joke was <u>witty</u>.
   serious   sad   (funny)

8. Jeff needs a <u>boost</u> to reach the water fountain.
   push   (lift)   drop

© Harcourt • Grade 2

▶ Write the two words that make up each
underlined contraction.

1. We'll visit the zoo. _____ We will
2. The zoo isn't far away. _____ is not
3. It's a place to see wild animals. _____ It is
4. Some animals aren't easy to see. _____ are not
5. They don't come out in daytime. _____ do not
6. They'll be sleeping underground. _____ They will
7. We shouldn't try to wake them. _____ should not
8. There's a sleeping animal. _____ There is
9. He's cozy and warm. _____ He is
10. They're going to sleep all day. _____ They are

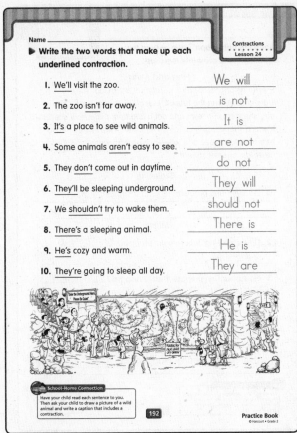

192

▶ Read the journal entry. Write *am*, *is*, *are*,
was, or *were* to complete each sentence.

March 15

Today we (1) ____ are ____ going to the zoo. I (2) ____ am ____ so
happy! When I (3) ____ was ____ four, my family went to the zoo.
We (4) ____ were ____ living in another city. Today (5) ____ is ____ the
first time we go to this zoo.

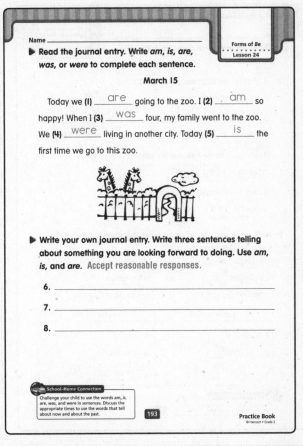

▶ Write your own journal entry. Write three sentences telling
about something you are looking forward to doing. Use *am*,
is, and *are*. **Accept reasonable responses.**

6. _____
7. _____
8. _____

193

▶ Circle and write the word in each sentence
that has the same vowel sound as *now*.

1. Please throw (out) the trash. _____ out
2. The (owl) has flown away. _____ owl
3. Do you live in this (house)? _____ house
4. A (crowd) watched the show. _____ crowd
5. Bo (found) a bowl to use. _____ found

▶ On the line, write the abbreviation for the underlined word.

6. Talia's dad is Mister Robbins. _____ Mr.
7. The ball game is on Saturday. _____ Sat.
8. Nia's birthday is in January. _____ Jan.
9. We go to Doctor Vargas. _____ Dr.
10. The store is on Main Street. _____ St.

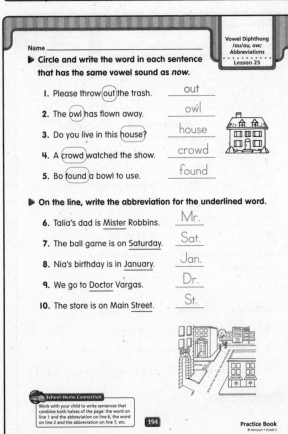

194

▶ Fold the paper along the dotted line. As
each spelling word is read, write it in the
blank. Then unfold your paper, and check
your work. Practice spelling any words
you missed.

1. _____
2. _____
3. _____
4. _____
5. _____
6. _____
7. _____
8. _____
9. _____
10. _____

Spelling Words

found
down
store
four
smooth
grew
true
fruit
care
pair

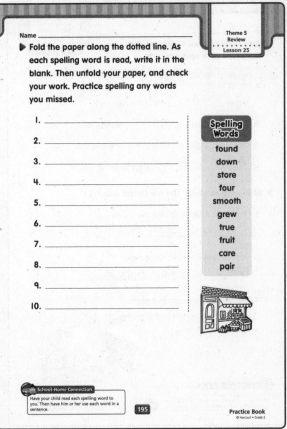

195

Name _____

▶ Circle the word that completes the sentence.

1. The runners dash around the race ____.

core (course) cars

2. Vic is too ____ to reach the shelf.

(short) shout shirt

3. Ivy ____ some milk into the glasses.

purrs (pours) pore

4. Big waves crash on the sandy ____.

(shore) share shower

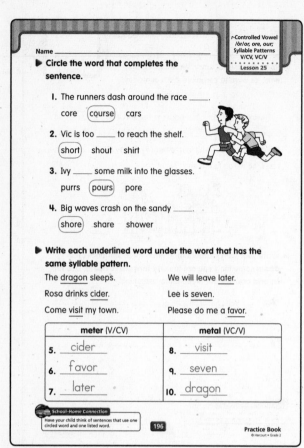

▶ Write each underlined word under the word that has the same syllable pattern.

The dragon sleeps.   We will leave later.

Rosa drinks cider.   Lee is seven.

Come visit my town.   Please do me a favor.

meter (V/CV)	metal (VC/V)
5. cider	8. visit
6. favor	9. seven
7. later	10. dragon

196

Name _____

▶ Read the paragraph. Then answer the questions and complete the chart.

Finn and Alvin

Finn the shepherd could not control her sheep. They wandered all over the hillside. Every day, they got lost. One day, she went into town and got a dog from the animal shelter. It was a sheepdog. Finn named him Alvin. Finn trained him to help herd the sheep and to keep them from wandering. Finn never lost another sheep!

Beginning

1. What is Finn's problem? Finn loses her sheep.

↓

Middle

2. How does Finn deal with the problem? Finn gets a sheepdog.

3. How does Finn prepare Alvin to help her? Finn trains Alvin to herd sheep.

↓

End

7. What happens in the end? Alvin helps Finn keep the sheep from wandering.

197

Name _____

▶ Write a verb from the box that best completes each sentence.

decide	listen	opens	talks

1. Robin _____talks_____ about the new park.

2. The town leaders _____decide_____ what to do.

3. They _____listen_____ to what the people want.

4. The park _____opens_____ on the Fourth of July.

▶ Write each sentence. Use the correct verb in ( ).

5. The council (serve, serves) the people.

The council serves the people.

6. Many towns (elect, elects) a mayor.

Many towns elect a mayor.

7. We (vote, votes) every two years.

We vote every two years.

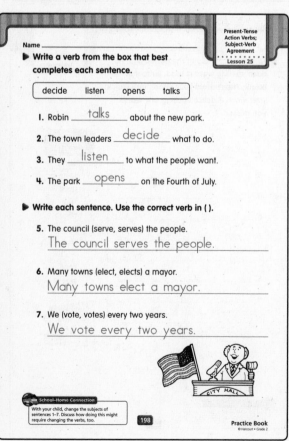

198

Name _____

▶ Finish the story. On each line, write a word from the box.

group	fruit	grew
smooth	blueberries	choose

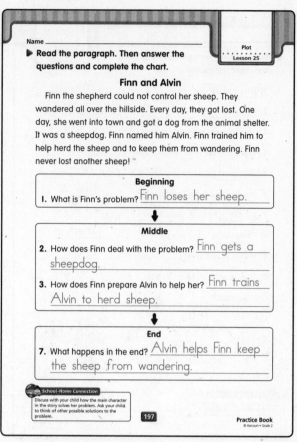

Hiking Harvest

Four friends hiked to a spot where bushes

(1) _____grew_____ close together. The

(2) _____group_____ carried pails. Everyone picked

(3) _____blueberries_____ from the bushes. The friends

were careful to (4) _____choose_____ only the ripe

ones. They planned to mix the berries with other kinds of

(5) _____fruit_____ in a tasty salad.

▶ Write a prefix from the box to complete the word in each sentence.

mis-	re-	un-

6. If you want more juice, __re__fill the glass.

7. I am __un__able to open the jar of glue.

8. Drew was in a bad mood and felt __un__happy.

9. Mr. Renfrow has __mis__placed his soup spoon and can't find it.

199

Student Edition pp. 196–199

Name ___

▶ **Read the passage. Think about how the characters are alike and different. Then fill in the Venn diagram.**

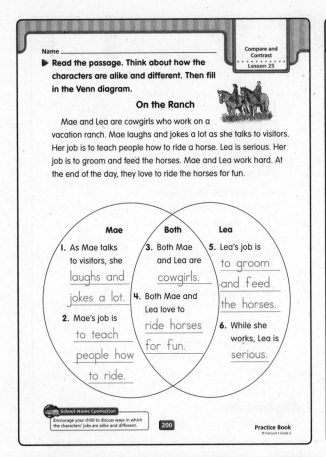

On the Ranch

Mae and Lea are cowgirls who work on a vacation ranch. Mae laughs and jokes a lot as she talks to visitors. Her job is to teach people how to ride a horse. Lea is serious. Her job is to groom and feed the horses. Mae and Lea work hard. At the end of the day, they love to ride the horses for fun.

Mae
1. As Mae talks to visitors, she laughs and jokes a lot.
2. Mae's job is to teach people how to ride.

Both
3. Both Mae and Lea are cowgirls.
4. Both Mae and Lea love to ride horses for fun.

Lea
5. Lea's job is to groom and feed the horses.
6. While she works, Lea is serious.

200

Name ___

▶ **Write the word that answers the question.**

1. Which word goes with accomplish? _task_
   game   task   sleep

2. Which word goes with serve? _help_
   help   show   make

3. Which word goes with attend? _party_
   party   test   store

4. Which word goes with area? _space_
   breath   chair   space

5. Which word goes with report? _tell_
   hear   tell   smell

6. Which word goes with feasible? _possible_
   pretend   chilly   possible

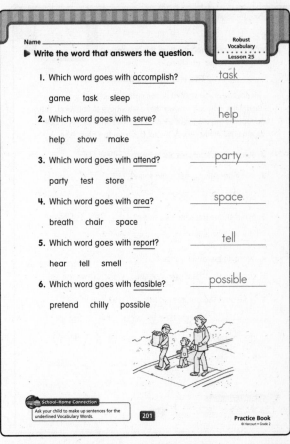

201

Name ___

▶ **Circle and write the word in each sentence that has the same vowel sound as *air*.**

1. Sit on a (chair) near the garden. _chair_

2. Do you hear a (pair) of buzzing bees? _pair_

3. If you (stare) hard, you may see a spider's web. _stare_

4. Try not to (scare) off the butterfly sipping nectar from a flower. _scare_

5. All sorts of living things are (sharing) this small patch of earth. _sharing_

▶ **Write the two words that make up each underlined contraction.**

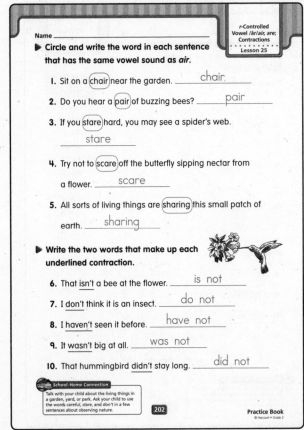

6. That isn't a bee at the flower. _is not_

7. I don't think it is an insect. _do not_

8. I haven't seen it before. _have not_

9. It wasn't big at all. _was not_

10. That hummingbird didn't stay long. _did not_

202

Name ___

▶ **Read each verb that tells about now. Change the verb to make it tell about the past.**

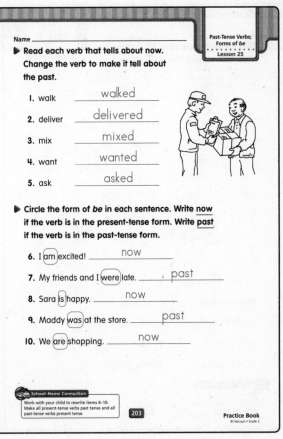

1. walk _walked_

2. deliver _delivered_

3. mix _mixed_

4. want _wanted_

5. ask _asked_

▶ **Circle the form of *be* in each sentence. Write now if the verb is in the present-tense form. Write past if the verb is in the past-tense form.**

6. I (am) excited! _now_

7. My friends and I (were) late. _past_

8. Sara (is) happy. _now_

9. Maddy (was) at the store. _past_

10. We (are) shopping. _now_

203

The Honeybee's Dance

Name _____

▶ Read the paragraph. Look at the diagram. Then answer the questions.

Use Graphic Aids
Lesson 25

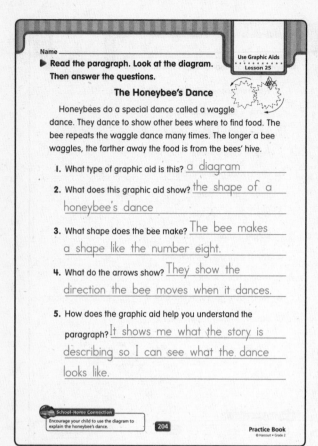

Honeybees do a special dance called a waggle dance. They dance to show other bees where to find food. The bee repeats the waggle dance many times. The longer a bee waggles, the farther away the food is from the bees' hive.

1. What type of graphic aid is this? _a diagram_

2. What does this graphic aid show? _the shape of a honeybee's dance_

3. What shape does the bee make? _The bee makes a shape like the number eight._

4. What do the arrows show? _They show the direction the bee moves when it dances._

5. How does the graphic aid help you understand the paragraph? _It shows me what the story is describing so I can see what the dance looks like._

School-Home Connection
Encourage your child to use the diagram to explain the honeybee's dance.

204

Practice Book
© Harcourt • Grade 2

Name _____

▶ Read the questions. Circle the correct answer.

Synonyms
Lesson 25

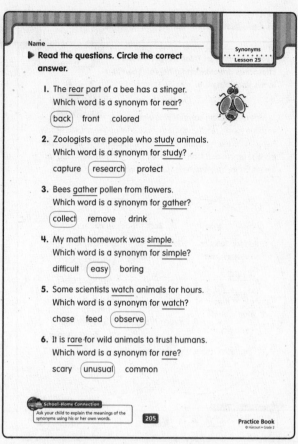

1. The rear part of a bee has a stinger. Which word is a synonym for rear?
   (back)   front   colored

2. Zoologists are people who study animals. Which word is a synonym for study?
   capture   (research)   protect

3. Bees gather pollen from flowers. Which word is a synonym for gather?
   (collect)   remove   drink

4. My math homework was simple. Which word is a synonym for simple?
   difficult   (easy)   boring

5. Some scientists watch animals for hours. Which word is a synonym for watch?
   chase   feed   (observe)

6. It is rare for wild animals to trust humans. Which word is a synonym for rare?
   scary   (unusual)   common

School-Home Connection
Ask your child to explain the meanings of the synonyms using his or her own words.

205

Practice Book
© Harcourt • Grade 2

Name _____

▶ Read the sentences. Write the letter of the sentence that goes with each picture.

Vowel Variant
/ŏŏ/ oo, ou
Lesson 26

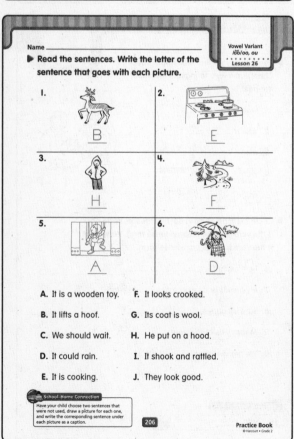

1. B	2. E
3. H	4. F
5. A	6. D

A. It is a wooden toy.
B. It lifts a hoof.
C. We should wait.
D. It could rain.
E. It is cooking.

F. It looks crooked.
G. Its coat is wool.
H. He put on a hood.
I. It shook and rattled.
J. They look good.

School-Home Connection
Have your child choose two sentences that were not used, draw a picture for each one, and write the corresponding sentence under each picture as a caption.

206

Practice Book
© Harcourt • Grade 2

Name _____

▶ Read the Spelling Words. Sort them and write them where they belong.

Vowel Variants
/ŏŏ/ oo, ou
Lesson 26

Order may vary.

Words with oo

1. _book_
2. _took_
3. _stood_
4. _crook_
5. _look_
6. _good_
7. _shook_

Words with ou

8. _should_
9. _would_
10. _could_

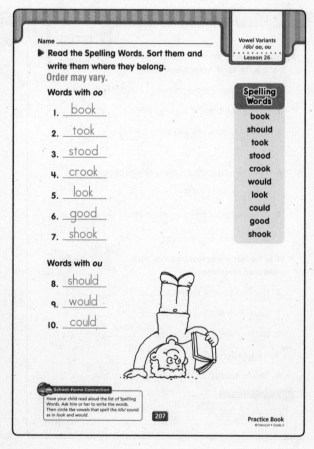

Spelling Words

book
should
took
stood
crook
would
look
could
good
shook

School-Home Connection
Have your child read aloud the list of Spelling Words. Ask him or her to write the words. Then circle the vowels that spell the /ŏŏ/ sound as in look and would.

207

Practice Book
© Harcourt • Grade 2

© Harcourt • Grade 2

▶ Read the story. Then, in the chart, write a sentence to tell a cause or an effect.

Mandy's Sunhat

"My hat has a hole!" said Mandy. So Mandy and Mom went shopping.

Mandy tried on a dark pink hat. Pink was Mandy's favorite color. Mom did not buy the hat, because it was too floppy. Mandy tried on a light pink hat with beads. Mom did not buy the hat, because it was too expensive. At last, Mandy tried on a bright pink hat with a yellow flower.

"It's perfect!" said Mandy. Mom bought the hat.

Cause	Effect
1. Mandy needed a new hat.	Mandy and Mom went shopping.
2. Pink is Mandy's favorite color.	Mandy tried on pink hats.
3. The dark pink hat was too floppy.	Mom did not buy the dark pink hat.
4. The light pink hat was too expensive.	Mom did not buy the light pink hat.
5. The hat with the flower was perfect.	Mom bought the hat with the flower.

School-Home Connection
Discuss what children do in the morning to get ready for school. Ask your child to explain the causes and effects of his or her own experiences.

208

Practice Book
© Harcourt • Grade 2

▶ Circle and write the word that completes each sentence.

1. Stir the soup with a ___wooden___ spoon.
   (wooden)   wouldn't   woolen

2. Lou wrote in his new ___notebook___.
   bookcase   bookstore   (notebook)

3. The wind blew, and houses ___shook___.
   hooks   (shook)   hoods

4. Cooper ___stood___ on a stool to reach the shelf.
   (stood)   crooked   looking

5. We came as soon as we ___could___.
   (could)   cold   club

6. Can you hear the sounds of horse ___hoofbeats___?
   goodness   lookouts   (hoofbeats)

7. We ___understood___ the rules of the game.
   should   (understood)   handbook

8. Boone may choose to run in a ___footrace___.
   footprint   (footrace)   firewood

School-Home Connection
Ask your child to copy all the words with oo or ou, and list them by shared vowel sound.

209

Practice Book
© Harcourt • Grade 2

▶ Circle the answer to each question.

1. What might pancakes be **smothered** with?
   flour   (syrup)   a dish

2. Which words show that the speaker **pleaded**?
   ("Please help me.")   "I'm busy now."   "Who are you?"

3. What could be **fragrant**?
   loud music   (freshly-baked bread)   a clear glass bowl

4. What moves **gently**?
   crashing sea waves   a race car   (a soft breeze)

5. How can you tell that someone **grunted**?
   You see footprints.
   You smell sweet flowers.
   (You hear a low sound.)

6. If you **replied**, what did you do?
   (answered)   questioned   moved again

7. How can you tell if a flower is **fragrant**?
   touch it   (smell it)   look at it

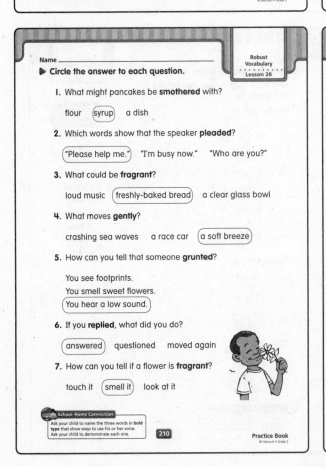

School-Home Connection
Ask your child to name the three words in bold type that show ways to use his or her voice. Ask your child to demonstrate each one.

210

Practice Book
© Harcourt • Grade 2

▶ Circle the word that is an antonym for the underlined word. Then write it on the line to complete the sentence.

1. Seth sent the letter, and Andy ___received___ it.
   caught   found   (received)

2. Angie felt better but May felt ___worse___.
   sadder   (worse)   happier

3. One airplane landed while another ___took off___.
   (took off)   parked   flew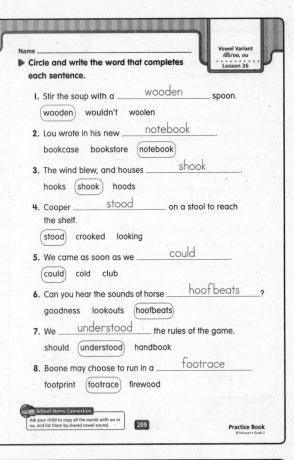

4. I lost my pencil but I ___found___ my paintbrush.
   sharpened   dropped   (found)

5. Katie pushed the cart, and Jason ___pulled___ it.
   shoved   (pulled)   cleaned

6. I got three answers right and one ___wrong___.
   correct   hard   (wrong)

7. That question is easy. I know the ___answer___.
   problem   (answer)   number

School-Home Connection
Help your child think of antonyms for some of the other words on this page.

211

Practice Book
© Harcourt • Grade 2

Student Edition pp. 208–211

Name _____

▶ Write the prefix from the box to complete the word in each sentence.

| dis-   over-   pre- |

1. Before Rosa began kindergarten at this **school**, she went to a __pre__ school.

2. I **like** most fruits, but I __dis__ like lemons because they taste too sour.

3. The library book was **due** last Monday, so it is now __over__ due.

4. Before the plane took off on its **flight**, the __pre__ flight check was done.

5. Our dog **obeys**, but once in a while, she __dis__ obeys.

6. The friends **agreed** to play the game, but they __dis__ agreed about who should go first.

7. **Cook** the beans for only a short time, and do not __over__ cook them.

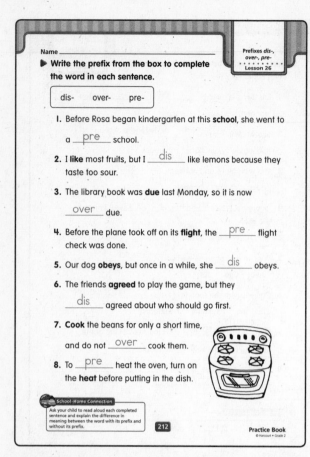

8. To __pre__ heat the oven, turn on the **heat** before putting in the dish.

School-Home Connection
Ask your child to read aloud each completed sentence and explain the difference in meaning between the word with its prefix and without its prefix.

212

Practice Book
© Harcourt • Grade 2

Name _____

▶ Read each sentence. If *has, had,* or *have* is used correctly, write *yes*. If the verb is not used correctly, write *no*.

1. I has a bucket. __no__

2. I have a shovel, too. __yes__

3. We had fun this morning. __yes__

4. We has a picnic on the sand. __no__

5. Jasmine have seven seashells. __no__

▶ Rewrite the sentences that are incorrect above. Write them correctly on the lines.

6. I have a bucket.

7. We had a picnic on the sand.

8. Jasmine has seven seashells.

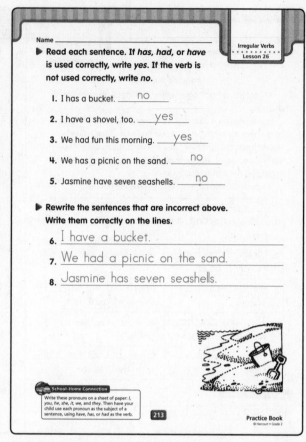

School-Home Connection
Write these pronouns on a sheet of paper: *I, you, he, she, it, we,* and *they.* Then have your child use each pronoun as the subject of a sentence, using *have, has,* or *had* as the verb.

213

Practice Book
© Harcourt • Grade 2

Name _____

▶ Circle the word that goes with each picture.

1. 	2.	3.
yawn **your** yank	pours **paws** pass	court **caught** cookout
4.	**5.**	**6.**
straw strap stray	**crawl** claw crow	**drawing** drown dawn
7.	**8.**	**9.**
raw law **jaw**	lunch **launch** lance	grown awning **lawn**
10.	**11.**	**12.**
swinging sowing **seesaw**	howl haul **hawk**	show **claw** flew

School-Home Connection
Have your child copy all the words with *au* or *aw* that are on this page. Ask your child to read them aloud and tell what each one means.

214

Practice Book
© Harcourt • Grade 2

Name _____

▶ Read the Spelling Words. Sort the words and write them where they belong.
Order may vary.

Words with *aw*

1. claw
2. draw
3. crawl
4. lawn
5. paw
6. saw

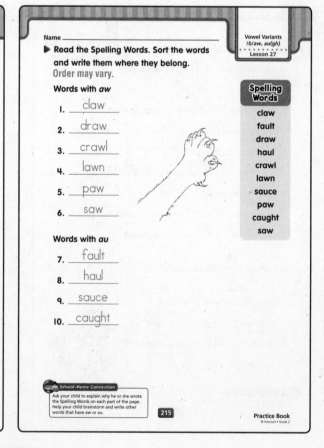

Words with *au*

7. fault
8. haul
9. sauce
10. caught

Spelling Words

claw
fault
draw
haul
crawl
lawn
sauce
paw
caught
saw

School-Home Connection
Ask your child to explain why he or she wrote the Spelling Words on each part of the page. Help your child brainstorm and write other words that have *aw* or *au.*

215

Practice Book
© Harcourt • Grade 2

© Harcourt • Grade 2

Name _____

▶ Read the biography. Then complete the chart.

Arnold Lobel

When Arnold Lobel was young he loved to draw and make up stories for his friends. When he grew up, he became a writer and illustrator. He watched cartoons to know what kinds of stories children like. Arnold Lobel wrote the Frog and Toad books because he believed learning to read should be fun. His first book, Frog and Toad Are Friends, was a big hit. It won many honors, and children still love reading it.

Cause	Effect
1. He liked to draw and make up stories.	Arnold Lobel became a writer and an illustrator.
2. He wanted to know the kinds of stories kids like.	He watched cartoons.
Arnold Lobel believed learning to read should be fun.	3. He wrote the Frog and Toad series.
Everyone loved reading Frog and Toad Are Friends.	4. It won many honors.

School-Home Connection
Discuss the causes and effects with your child. Ask him or her to explain how the causes and effect are linked.

216

Practice Book
© Harcourt • Grade 2

Name _____

▶ Finish the story. On each line, write a word from the box.

author	drawing	taught	caught
claws	hawk	saw	because

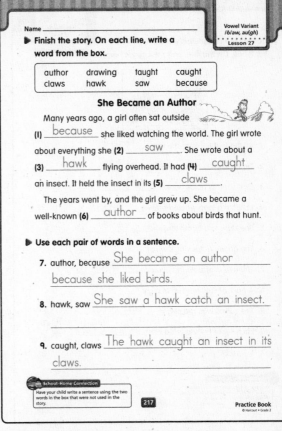

She Became an Author

Many years ago, a girl often sat outside

(1) _because_ she liked watching the world. The girl wrote

about everything she (2) _saw_. She wrote about a

(3) _hawk_ flying overhead. It had (4) _caught_

an insect. It held the insect in its (5) _claws_.

The years went by, and the girl grew up. She became a

well-known (6) _author_ of books about birds that hunt.

▶ Use each pair of words in a sentence.

7. author, because _She became an author_ _because she liked birds._

8. hawk, saw _She saw a hawk catch an insect._

9. caught, claws _The hawk caught an insect in its_ _claws._

School-Home Connection
Have your child write a sentence using the two words in the box that were not used in the story.

217

Practice Book
© Harcourt • Grade 2

Name _____

▶ Write two words from the box that go with each Vocabulary Word. Write the words on the lines below the Vocabulary Word.

read	prize	important	imagine
build	wonderful	saw	distant
sensed	study	farther	trophy

1. beyond _distant_ _farther_

2. create _imagine_ _build_

3. literature _read_ _study_

4. noticed _saw_ _sensed_

5. award _prize_ _trophy_

6. grand _important_ _wonderful_

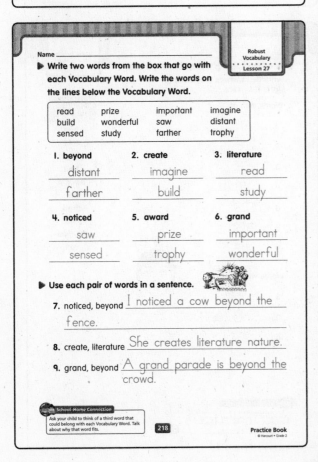

▶ Use each pair of words in a sentence.

7. noticed, beyond _I noticed a cow beyond the_ _fence._

8. create, literature _She creates literature nature._

9. grand, beyond _A grand parade is beyond the_ _crowd._

School-Home Connection
Ask your child to think of a third word that could belong with each Vocabulary Word. Talk about why that word fits.

218

Practice Book
© Harcourt • Grade 2

Name _____

▶ Circle the word that is an antonym for the underlined word in the sentence. Then write the antonym to complete the sentence.

1. Mom loves the summer, but she _hates_ the winter.
   likes   enjoys   (hates)

2. Liam saw a beautiful flower and an _ugly_ toad.
   sad   (ugly)   pretty

3. The puppy was asleep, but the kitten was _awake_.
   (awake)   excited   furry

4. I caught the ball, but Rita _missed_ it.
   carried   held   (missed)

5. Tim created a sand castle, but his little sister _destroyed_ it.
   built   (destroyed)   cleaned

6. The cat was outside, but the parrot was _inside_.
   above   below   (inside)

School-Home Connection
Encourage your child to write antonyms for the words not circled under each sentence.

219

Practice Book
© Harcourt • Grade 2

© Harcourt • Grade 2

Student Edition pp. 216–219

Name _____

▶ Correct the underlined word in each sentence. On the line, write the correct word.

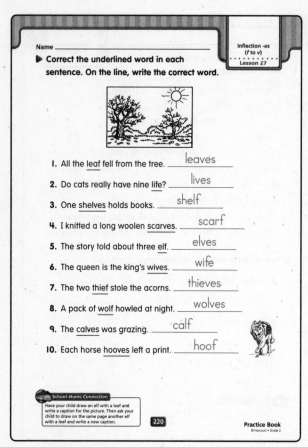

1. All the leaf fell from the tree. __leaves__

2. Do cats really have nine life? __lives__

3. One shelves holds books. __shelf__

4. I knitted a long woolen scarves. __scarf__

5. The story told about three elf. __elves__

6. The queen is the king's wives. __wife__

7. The two thief stole the acorns. __thieves__

8. A pack of wolf howled at night. __wolves__

9. The calves was grazing. __calf__

10. Each horse hooves left a print. __hoof__

220

Practice Book
© Harcourt • Grade 2

Name _____

▶ Read each sentence. Draw one line under the verbs that tell about now and two lines under the verbs that tell about the past.

1. We go on a hike.

2. We run down the hills.

3. David came with us.

4. We saw fossils in the sand.

▶ 5.–8. Rewrite the story. Make each verb tell about now.

We came to Sunset Trail. Jake ran ahead of us. He saw a squirrel. We went to see the squirrel, too.

We come to Sunset Trail. Jake runs ahead of us. He sees a squirrel. We go to see the squirrel, too.

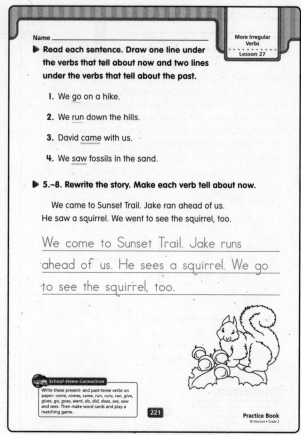

221

Practice Book
© Harcourt • Grade 2

Name _____

▶ Choose the word from the box that completes each rhyme.

| chalk | thought | halt | hall |
| tall | salt | talk | fought |

1. Doreen never __thought__

   That the ball would be caught.

2. I have a friend named Paul

   Who is very, very __tall__.

3. Do you think that a hawk

   Can be taught how to __talk__?

4. The baby would crawl

   Down the long, narrow __hall__.

5. I don't think it's my fault

   That I just spilled the __salt__.

6. The new teacher taught

   About wars that were __fought__.

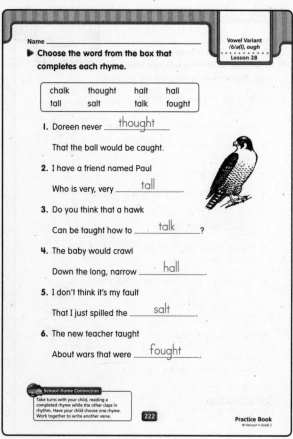

222

Practice Book
© Harcourt • Grade 2

Name _____

▶ Read the Spelling Words. Sort them and write them where they belong.
Order may vary.

Words with al

1. __ball__

2. __talk__

3. __hall__

4. __all__

5. __chalk__

6. __small__

7. __fall__

Words with ough

8. __fought__

9. __bought__

10. __thought__

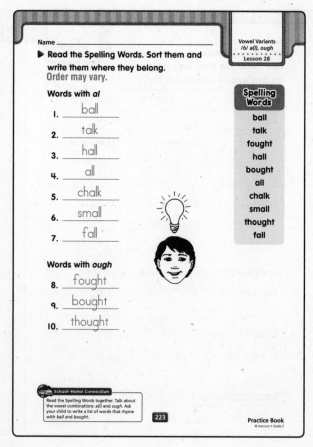

Spelling Words

ball
talk
fought
hall
bought
all
chalk
small
thought
fall

223

Practice Book
© Harcourt • Grade 2

© Harcourt • Grade 2

Name _____

▶ **Read the paragraph. Then complete the chart.**
Possible responses are shown.

One Hot Island

Red melted rock pours down the side of the mountain. At the bottom, the mountain looks like frozen cake batter. The ground is made of gray hardened rock. If you touch it, it still feels hot. Welcome to Hawaii, the land of smoking, hot mountains.

Detail	What I Know	Inference
Red melted rock pours down a mountain in Hawaii.	Volcanoes are mountains that pour out hot, melted rock when they erupt.	What is the author describing? watching a volcano in Hawaii.
At the bottom, the mountain looks like frozen cake batter.	Melted rock from a volcano can cool and become hard.	What is the author describing? the cooled hardened rock

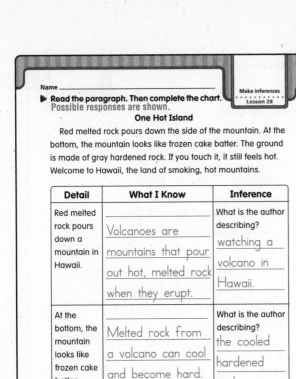

School–Home Connection
Ask your child to describe what it would be like to visit the place described in the paragraph. Ask your child to tell how he or she would feel.

224

Practice Book
© Harcourt • Grade 2

Name _____

▶ **Circle and write the word that completes each sentence.**

1. Leah _____thought_____ she would collect rocks.
   taught   thawed   (thought)

2. She _____bought_____ a book about rock collecting.
   (bought)   both   bowed

3. It was _____false_____ to think that all rocks are hard.
   face   fought   (false)

4. Leah was _____walking_____ in the woods, looking for rocks.
   waking   (walking)   weaken

5. Pine needles had _____fallen_____ onto the path.
   fawn   found   (fallen)

6. She looked up at the _____tall_____ pine trees.
   tail   (tall)   towel

7. Leah gave a _____talk_____ in her class about her rocks.
   (talk)   took   take

8. She told what each kind was _____called_____.
   caught   coiled   (called)

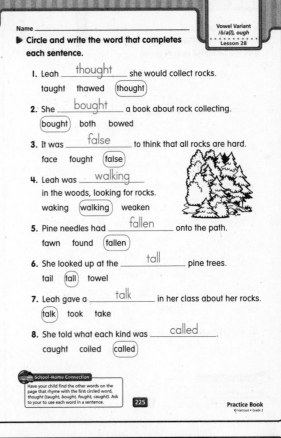

School–Home Connection
Have your child find the other words on the page that rhyme with the first circled word, thought (taught, bought, fought, caught). Ask to your to use each word in a sentence.

225

Practice Book
© Harcourt • Grade 2

Name _____

▶ **Circle the answer to each question.**

1. Which of these is rare?
   (four-leaf clover)   weed   gray pebble

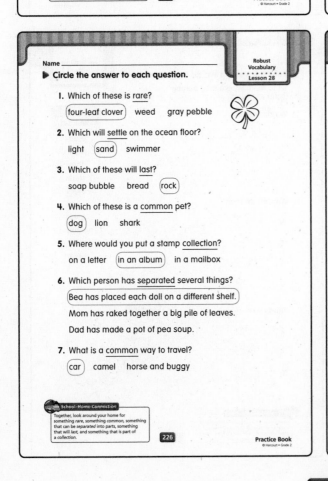

2. Which will settle on the ocean floor?
   light   (sand)   swimmer

3. Which of these will last?
   soap bubble   bread   (rock)

4. Which of these is a common pet?
   (dog)   lion   shark

5. Where would you put a stamp collection?
   on a letter   (in an album)   in a mailbox

6. Which person has separated several things?
   (Bea has placed each doll on a different shelf.)
   Mom has raked together a big pile of leaves.
   Dad has made a pot of pea soup.

7. What is a common way to travel?
   (car)   camel   horse and buggy

School–Home Connection
Together, look around your home for something rare, something common, something that can be separated into parts, something that will last, and something that is part of a collection.

226

Practice Book
© Harcourt • Grade 2

Name _____

▶ **Circle the correct meaning for each underlined word. Then write the meaning in the sentence.**

1. I was the first to spot a ladybug.
   Spot means _____to see_____
   a patch   (to see)

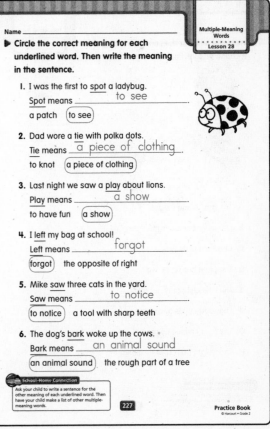

2. Dad wore a tie with polka dots.
   Tie means _____a piece of clothing_____
   to knot   (a piece of clothing)

3. Last night we saw a play about lions.
   Play means _____a show_____
   to have fun   (a show)

4. I left my bag at school!
   Left means _____forgot_____
   (forgot)   the opposite of right

5. Mike saw three cats in the yard.
   Saw means _____to notice_____
   (to notice)   a tool with sharp teeth

6. The dog's bark woke up the cows.
   Bark means _____an animal sound_____
   (an animal sound)   the rough part of a tree

School–Home Connection
Ask your child to write a sentence for the other meaning of each underlined word. Then have your child make a list of other multiple-meaning words.

227

Practice Book
© Harcourt • Grade 2

© Harcourt • Grade 2

Student Edition pp. 224–227

▶ **Write the letters that complete the word so that the sentence makes sense.**

1. This spy film has lots of ___ac___tion.

   ac   men   posi

2. Jeb added another rock to his ___collec___tion.

   cau   collec   cap

3. Please pay ___atten___tion in class.

   direc   atten   frac

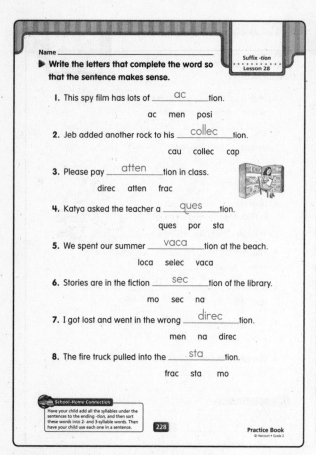

4. Katya asked the teacher a ___ques___tion.

   ques   por   sta

5. We spent our summer ___vaca___tion at the beach.

   loca   selec   vaca

6. Stories are in the fiction ___sec___tion of the library.

   mo   sec   na

7. I got lost and went in the wrong ___direc___tion.

   men   na   direc

8. The fire truck pulled into the ___sta___tion.

   frac   sta   mo

School–Home Connection
Have your child add all the syllables under the sentences to the ending -tion, and then sort these words into 2- and 3-syllable words. Then have your child use each one in a sentence.

228

Practice Book
© Harcourt • Grade 2

▶ **Rewrite each sentence, adding the helping verb *have* or *has*.**

1. Josh brought his bike to the store.

   Josh has brought his bike to the store.

2. He bought a special box.

   He has bought a special box.

3. I used a box for my toy cars.

   I have used a box for my toy cars.

4. My cars stayed together in the box.

   My cars have stayed together in the box.

▶ **Write each sentence. Use the correct helping verb in ( ).**

5. My father (have, has) given my mother a diamond ring.

   My father has given my mother a diamond ring.

6. I (has, have) tried it on.

   I have tried it on.

7. My mother (has, have) worn it for years.

   My mother has worn it for years.

8. I (has, have) always dreamed of wearing a diamond ring someday. I have always dreamed of wearing a diamond ring someday.

School–Home Connection
Talk with your child about the helping verbs on the page. Then have him or her generate sentences using each helping verb.

229

Practice Book
© Harcourt • Grade 2

Name _____

Long Vowel /ā/ea,
ei(gh), ey
Lesson 29

▶ **Write the letter of the sentence that goes with the picture.** Possible responses are shown.

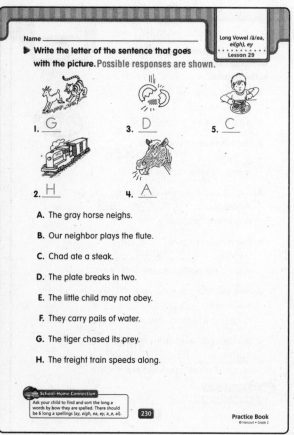

1. G

2. H

3. D

4. A

5. C

A. The gray horse neighs.

B. Our neighbor plays the flute.

C. Chad ate a steak.

D. The plate breaks in two.

E. The little child may not obey.

F. They carry pails of water.

G. The tiger chased its prey.

H. The freight train speeds along.

School–Home Connection
Ask your child to find and sort the long a words by how they are spelled. There should be 6 long a spellings (ay, eigh, ea, ey, a_e, ai).

230

Practice Book
© Harcourt • Grade 2

Name _____

Long Vowel /ā/ea,
ei(gh), ey
Lesson 29

▶ **Read the Spelling Words. Sort them and write them where they belong.**
Order may vary.

Words with *ea*

1. break

2. steak

3. great

Words with *eigh*

4. sleigh

5. eight

6. neighbor

7. weigh

Words with *ey*

8. they

9. obey

10. prey

Spelling Words

break
sleigh
they
steak
eight
obey
great
neighbor
prey
weigh

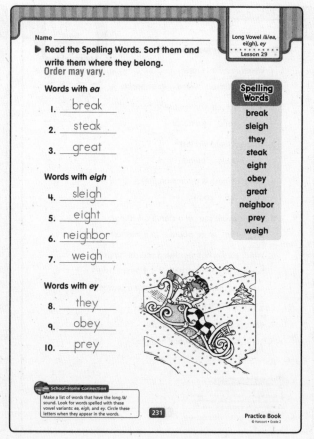

School–Home Connection
Make a list of words that have the long /ā/ sound. Look for words spelled with these vowel variants: ea, eigh, and ey. Circle these letters when they appear in the words.

231

Practice Book
© Harcourt • Grade 2

© Harcourt • Grade 2

▶ Read the story. Then finish the sentences to fill in the chart.

Harry's Special Place

Harry stuck his head out of the window. He could hear the clucking from around the corner of the house. Before long, there they were, pecking at the new seeds in the garden. Harry began barking excitedly. They just ignored him and kept pecking. Harry couldn't stand it anymore. He jumped out of the window and chased them into the barn. His tail wagged the whole way.

Details		What I Know		Inference
Harry began barking. Harry wagged his tail. Harry could hear clucking. They were pecking at the seeds in the garden. Harry chased them into the barn.	+	1. Dogs bark and wag their tails. 3. Chickens cluck and peck seeds. 5. Farms have barns.	=	2. Harry is a dog 4. The animals that Harry chases are chickens. 6. This story takes place on a farm

School-Home Connection
Have your child read the story to you. Then ask him or her which words describe what Harry is like.

232

Practice Book
© Harcourt • Grade 2

▶ Finish the story. On each line, write a word from the box.

break	neighborhood	they	eight
obey	weight	steak	neighbors
	great	prey	

Lizard Saves the Day!

Lizard was about to nap in the sun when she saw a fox sneaking around in her **(1)** ____neighborhood____ . She ran to warn her **(2)** ____neighbors____ .

She saw **(3)** ____eight____ rabbits nibbling grass beside their home. "Go back inside," she whispered, "or you'll become the fox's **(4)** ____prey____ !" Then she raced up a tree and hid herself.

The rabbits were quick to **(5)** ____obey____ her warning. Afterward, **(6)** ____they____ came back outside and looked for Lizard. "You are a

(7) ____great____ friend!" the littlest rabbit told her and gave her a hug.

School-Home Connection
Have your child read the finished story to you. Then ask your child to list words from the box that rhyme. Help your child think of other rhyming words to add to each list.

233

Practice Book
© Harcourt • Grade 2

▶ Write two words from the box to go with the Vocabulary Word.

whole	looked	racing	hurrying
find	grand	all	invention
stir	move	stared	proud

1. entire
   whole
   all

2. budge
   stir
   move

3. majestic
   grand
   proud

4. scampering
   racing
   hurrying

5. peered
   looked
   stared

6. discovery
   find
   invention

▶ Use each pair of words in a sentence.

7. peered, entire I peered out of the window and saw the entire sky filled with stars.

8. budge, scampering My kitten wouldn't budge, but then he went scampering away.

School-Home Connection
Have your child choose one sentence from 7 or 8 to illustrate.

234

Practice Book
© Harcourt • Grade 2

▶ Circle and write the correct meaning for the underlined word. Then write the meaning on the line.

1. The leaves turn colors in the fall.
   Here, fall means a season of the year
   to trip   (a season of the year)

2. I store my toys in the closet.
   Here, store means keep
   (keep)   a place where you buy things

3. The doctor examined my chest.
   Here, chest means a part of the body
   a large box   (a part of the body)

4. That's not the right answer.
   Here, right means correct
   (correct)   the opposite of left

5. There was a long line outside the movie theater.
   Here, line means a row of people
   (a row of people)   a stripe you can draw

School-Home Connection
Encourage your child to write sentences using the other meanings of the words.

235

Practice Book
© Harcourt • Grade 2

Student Edition pp. 232–235

© Harcourt • Grade 2

Name _____

▶ **Add the ending -er or -est to the base word to finish the sentence. Write the word on the line.**

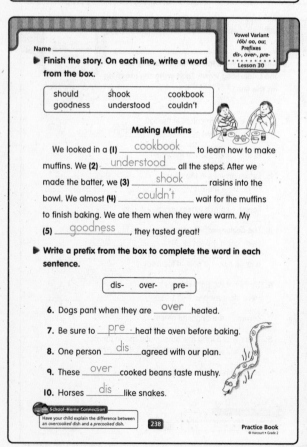

1. At first, the sun was shining its

   very _____brightest_____.   **bright**

2. Then it began to feel _____sleepier_____ than it ever had before.   **sleepy**

3. Slowly, the sun's light began

   to get _____dimmer_____.   **dim**

4. Soon, it was the _____darkest_____ day that anyone had ever seen.   **dark**

5. The _____finest_____ singers in the land quickly gathered.   **fine**

6. They sang loudly, and then they sang

   even _____louder_____.   **loud**

7. The sky began to get _____lighter_____ as the sun woke up.   **light**

School-Home Connection
Take turns pointing to objects you can see:
something small, something smaller, the
smallest object you can see. Spell each word.
Do the same with big, wide, and soft.

236

Practice Book
© Harcourt • Grade 2

Name _____

▶ **Read the paragraph. Make a contraction with the words in ( ). Write it on the line.**

I (would not) (1) _____wouldn't_____ like it if the sun did not come up. I (do not) (2) _____don't_____ like it when it is cold and dark. At those times, I (can not) (3) _____can't_____ see the flowers and trees. I am glad that the sun (does not) (4) _____doesn't_____ really disappear!

▶ **Write the two words that make up the contraction found in each sentence.**

5. Arlene Jameson hasn't gone to the lake.

   _____has not_____

6. She doesn't know how to get there. _____does not_____

7. The Jameson's weren't going to the lake.

   _____were not_____

8. We can't take Arlene with us. _____can not_____

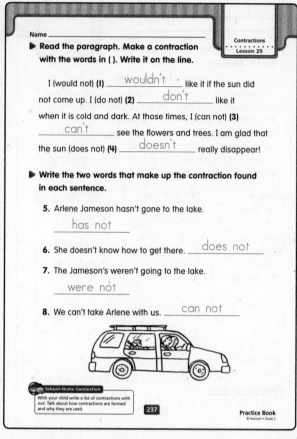

School-Home Connection
With your child write a list of contractions with
not. Talk about how contractions are formed
and why they are used.

237

Practice Book
© Harcourt • Grade 2

Vowel Variant
/ŏŏ/ oo, ou;
Prefixes
dis-, over-, pre-
Lesson 30

Name _____

▶ **Finish the story. On each line, write a word from the box.**

| should | shook | cookbook |
| goodness | understood | couldn't |

Making Muffins

We looked in a (1) _____cookbook_____ to learn how to make muffins. We (2) _____understood_____ all the steps. After we made the batter, we (3) _____shook_____ raisins into the bowl. We almost (4) _____couldn't_____ wait for the muffins to finish baking. We ate them when they were warm. My (5) _____goodness_____, they tasted great!

▶ **Write a prefix from the box to complete the word in each sentence.**

| dis- | over- | pre- |

6. Dogs pant when they are _____over_____heated.

7. Be sure to _____pre_____heat the oven before baking.

8. One person _____dis_____agreed with our plan.

9. These _____over_____cooked beans taste mushy.

10. Horses _____dis_____like snakes.

School-Home Connection
Have your child explain the difference between
an overcooked dish and a precooked dish.

238

Practice Book
© Harcourt • Grade 2

Name _____

▶ **Fold the paper along the dotted line. As each spelling word is read, write it in the blank. Then unfold your paper, and check your work. Practice spelling any words you missed.**

1. _____

2. _____

3. _____

4. _____

5. _____

6. _____

7. _____

8. _____

9. _____

10. _____

Spelling Words

took
should
draw
caught
fought
all
chalk
steak
neighbor
great

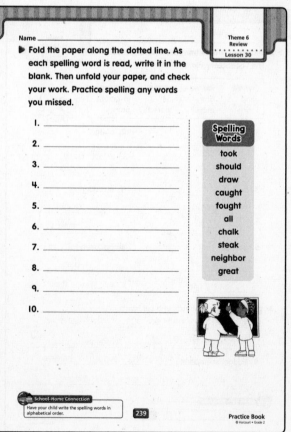

School-Home Connection
Have your child write the spelling words in
alphabetical order.

239

Practice Book
© Harcourt • Grade 2

© Harcourt • Grade 2

**Vowel Variant /ô/aw, au(gh); Inflection -es (f to v)
Lesson 30**

▶ Circle and write the word that completes the sentence.

1. The parents have a ___daughter___ and a son.
   dawn   drawing   (daughter)

2. We enjoyed our picnic on the ___lawn___.
   launch   (lawn)   laundry

3. The ___author___ wrote a new book.
   awning   (author)   awful

4. Shawn ___caught___ a bad cold.
   (caught)   because   fault

5. Look at the ___claws___ on that crab!
   (claws)   sauce   cause

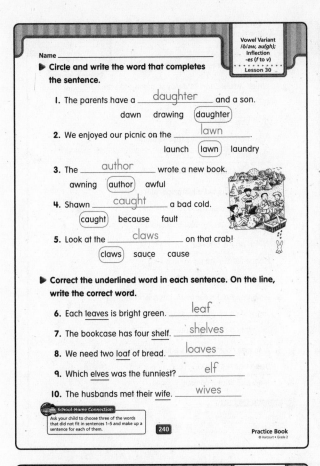

▶ Correct the underlined word in each sentence. On the line, write the correct word.

6. Each <u>leaves</u> is bright green. ___leaf___

7. The bookcase has four <u>shelf</u>. ___shelves___

8. We need two <u>loaf</u> of bread. ___loaves___

9. Which <u>elves</u> was the funniest? ___elf___

10. The husbands met their <u>wife</u>. ___wives___

240

Practice Book
© Harcourt • Grade 2

**Cause and Effect
Lesson 30**

▶ Read the story. Then fill in the chart to show causes or effects.

Visiting Grandma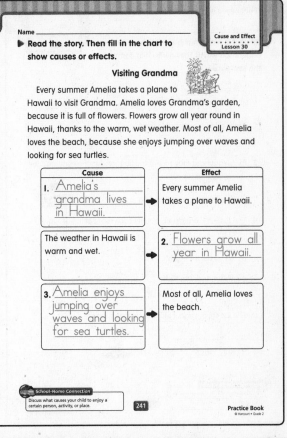

Every summer Amelia takes a plane to Hawaii to visit Grandma. Amelia loves Grandma's garden, because it is full of flowers. Flowers grow all year round in Hawaii, thanks to the warm, wet weather. Most of all, Amelia loves the beach, because she enjoys jumping over waves and looking for sea turtles.

Cause	Effect
1. Amelia's grandma lives in Hawaii.	Every summer Amelia takes a plane to Hawaii.
The weather in Hawaii is warm and wet.	2. Flowers grow all year in Hawaii.
3. Amelia enjoys jumping over waves and looking for sea turtles.	Most of all, Amelia loves the beach.

241

Practice Book
© Harcourt • Grade 2

**Irregular Verbs
Lesson 30**

▶ Write each sentence. Use the correct verb in ( ).

1. Jenny (have, has) pictures from her trip.
   Jenny has pictures from her trip.

2. Pat (goes, went) to the beach last year.
   Pat went to the beach last year.

3. I like to (run, ran) on the beach.
   I like to run on the beach.

4. We (do, does) many things on vacation.
   We do many things on vacation.

▶ Read the sentences that tell about now. Rewrite them to tell about the past.

5. Terry runs after a butterfly.
   Terry ran after a butterfly.

6. Nicki sees the mountains.
   Nicki saw the mountains.

7. Jessie goes surfing.
   Jessie went surfing.

242

Practice Book
© Harcourt • Grade 2

**Vowel Variant /ô/ a(l), ough; Suffix -tion
Lesson 30**

▶ Circle and write a word to complete the sentence.

1. Esi put some ___salt___ on her scrambled eggs.
   sought   (salt)   saw

2. The runners ___fought___ for the lead in the race.
   fault   fall   (fought)

3. Mr. Lee has lots of hair, but Mr. Fox is ___bald___.
   (bald)   bought   bold

4. Abby wanted to ___talk___ about the book she'd read.
   tall   took   (talk)

▶ Write the letters that complete the word in the sentence.

5. The train pulled into the ___sta___tion.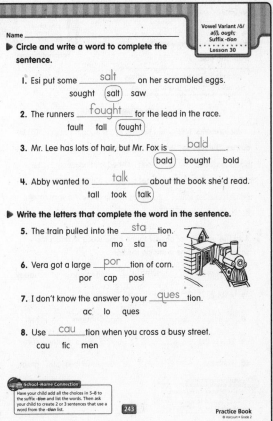
   mo   sta   na

6. Vera got a large ___por___tion of corn.
   por   cap   posi

7. I don't know the answer to your ___ques___tion.
   ac   lo   ques

8. Use ___cau___tion when you cross a busy street.
   cau   fic   men

243

Practice Book
© Harcourt • Grade 2

▶ **Circle the word that is an antonym for the underlined word. Then write it to complete the sentence.**

1. The game started at nine, and _____finished_____ at ten.

    began   ran   (finished)

2. Mom gave me an apple, and I _____took_____ it.

    threw   (took)   saved

3. In the morning they raised the flag, and in the evening they _____lowered_____ it.

    (lowered)   moved   washed

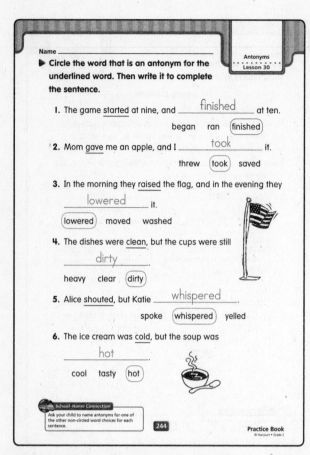

4. The dishes were clean, but the cups were still _____dirty_____.

    heavy   clear   (dirty)

5. Alice shouted, but Katie _____whispered_____.

    spoke   (whispered)   yelled

6. The ice cream was cold, but the soup was _____hot_____.

    cool   tasty   (hot)

School-Home Connection
Ask your child to name antonyms for one of the other non-circled word choices for each sentence.

244

Practice Book
© Harcourt • Grade 2

▶ **Circle the answer to the question.**

1. Which would cause a **delay** in getting to school?

    Gil got up early.

    (Lil got up late.)

2. Which one saw an **impressive** sight?

    (Tara saw the Grand Canyon.)

    Clara saw a bird flying.

3. Which one visited a **historical** place?

    Jim went to Blast Amusement Park.

    (Kim went to a Civil War battlefield.)

4. Which one is **upbeat**?

    (Happy Neal is eager to go hiking.)

    Gloomy Nell dreads going hiking.

5. Which one did a **fantastic** job raking leaves?

    Jody raked up half the leaves.

    (Toby raked up all the leaves.)

6. Who has cookies to **spare** for a dozen kids?

    Dean has ten cookies.

    (Jean has fifteen cookies.)

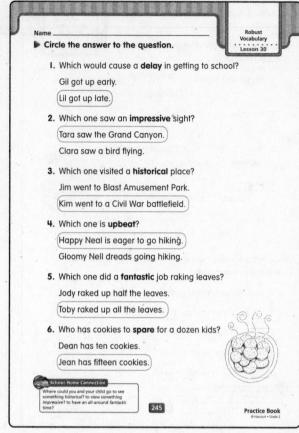

School-Home Connection
Where could you and your child go to see something *historical*? to view something *impressive*? to have an all-around *fantastic* time?

245

Practice Book
© Harcourt • Grade 2

▶ **Finish the story. On each line, write a word from the box.**

Long Vowel /ā/
ea, ei(gh), ey;
Inflections -er, -est
Lesson 30

| obeys | eight | break |
| steak | neighbors | they |

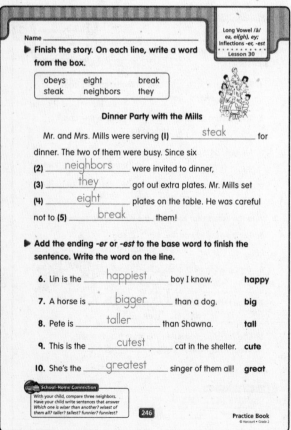

Dinner Party with the Mills

Mr. and Mrs. Mills were serving (1) _____steak_____ for dinner. The two of them were busy. Since six

(2) _____neighbors_____ were invited to dinner,

(3) _____they_____ got out extra plates. Mr. Mills set

(4) _____eight_____ plates on the table. He was careful not to (5) _____break_____ them!

▶ **Add the ending -er or -est to the base word to finish the sentence. Write the word on the line.**

6. Lin is the _____happiest_____ boy I know. **happy**

7. A horse is _____bigger_____ than a dog. **big**

8. Pete is _____taller_____ than Shawna. **tall**

9. This is the _____cutest_____ cat in the shelter. **cute**

10. She's the _____greatest_____ singer of them all! **great**

School-Home Connection
With your child, compare three neighbors. Have your child write sentences that answer *Which one is wiser than another? wisest of them all? taller? tallest? funnier? funniest?*

246

Practice Book
© Harcourt • Grade 2

▶ **Read the sentences. Circle the main verb. Underline the helping verb.**

1. My family has (visited) the Grand Canyon.

2. We have (hiked) in the mountains.

3. Dad had (climbed) to the top.

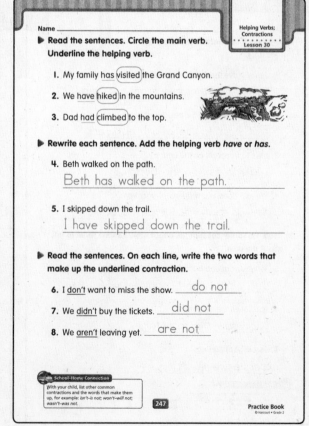

▶ **Rewrite each sentence. Add the helping verb *have* or *has*.**

4. Beth walked on the path.

    Beth has walked on the path.

5. I skipped down the trail.

    I have skipped down the trail.

▶ **Read the sentences. On each line, write the two words that make up the underlined contraction.**

6. I don't want to miss the show. _____do not_____

7. We didn't buy the tickets. _____did not_____

8. We aren't leaving yet. _____are not_____

School-Home Connection
With your child, list other common contractions and the words that make them up, for example: *isn't–is not; won't–will not; wasn't–was not.*

247

Practice Book
© Harcourt • Grade 2

© Harcourt • Grade 2

Student Edition pp. 244–247

▶ **Read the paragraph. Then complete the chart.** Possible responses are shown.

Diamonds for Everyone

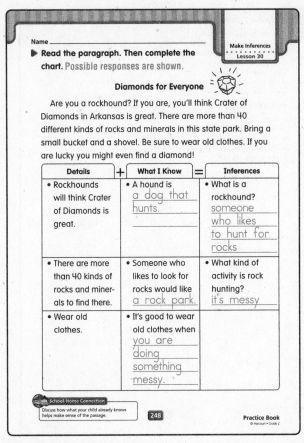

Are you a rockhound? If you are, you'll think Crater of Diamonds in Arkansas is great. There are more than 40 different kinds of rocks and minerals in this state park. Bring a small bucket and a shovel. Be sure to wear old clothes. If you are lucky you might even find a diamond!

Details	+	What I Know	=	Inferences
• Rockhounds will think Crater of Diamonds is great.		• A hound is a dog that hunts.		• What is a rockhound? someone who likes to hunt for rocks
• There are more than 40 kinds of rocks and minerals to find there.		• Someone who likes to look for rocks would like a rock park.		• What kind of activity is rock hunting? it's messy
• Wear old clothes.		• It's good to wear old clothes when you are doing something messy.		

School-Home Connection
Discuss how what your child already knows helps make sense of the passage.

248

Practice Book
© Harcourt • Grade 2

▶ **Circle and write the correct meaning for each underlined word.**

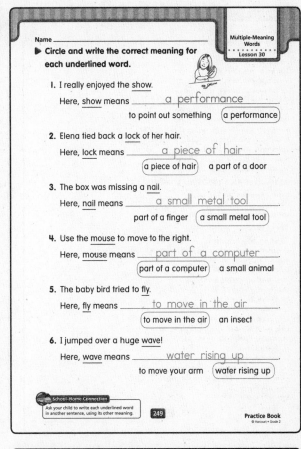

1. I really enjoyed the show.

   Here, show means ___a performance___

   to point out something   (a performance)

2. Elena tied back a lock of her hair.

   Here, lock means ___a piece of hair___

   (a piece of hair)   a part of a door

3. The box was missing a nail.

   Here, nail means ___a small metal tool___

   part of a finger   (a small metal tool)

4. Use the mouse to move to the right.

   Here, mouse means ___part of a computer___

   (part of a computer)   a small animal

5. The baby bird tried to fly.

   Here, fly means ___to move in the air___

   (to move in the air)   an insect

6. I jumped over a huge wave!

   Here, wave means ___water rising up___

   to move your arm   (water rising up)

School-Home Connection
Ask your child to write each underlined word in another sentence, using its other meaning.

249

Practice Book
© Harcourt • Grade 2

Index

250

Practice Book
© Harcourt • Grade 2

251

Practice Book
© Harcourt • Grade 2

Student Edition pp. 248–251

Practice Book
© Harcourt • Grade 2

Practice Book
© Harcourt • Grade 2

Student Edition pp. 252–253